Self Help Slut: Starting with a Clean Slate

By Katharine Branham

Katharine Branham

Published by Your Divine Birthright Publishers
7 Switchbud Place, Ste 192-279
The Woodlands, TX 77380
Phone: 888-568-3380; fax: 888-594-1244
www.ydbpublishers.com

First Edition

Editorial: Nikki T.

Cover/Interior Design: Your Divine Birthright Publishers

Illustrations: Katharine Branham

ISBN 978-1-956925-01-2

Library of Congress Control Number: 2022907610

Dedication

This workbook series is for every being that recognizes there is so much more and is ready to walk the path.

Katharine Branham

CONTENTS

Katharine Branham

Dear Sisters and Brothers,

There's no one else who can walk your spiritual path for you. When the timing is right, we will each be led to start down our individual paths on Earth. The fact that your soul signed up for the human experience is a testament to your will to reunite with the creator. Your choice to progress spiritually is seen as an etheric accolade carried in the energy field—one that will travel with you through eternity. It's seen by all the souls you cross paths with as well as those who have not acquired it. This auspicious accolade is a badge of courage for all other souls to admire.

I love you all,
Katharine

Katharine Branham

Self Help Slut: Starting with a Clean Slate

Katharine Branham

Starting with a Clean Slate

The Introduction

I 've had a few people very dear to me ask why I would want to write a workbook series helping readers clear the energy field. They've also been curious about the title I chose.

The title *Self Help Slut* came to me during a writing class I was taking when one of the other students was reading and his microphone was fading in and out. While he was adjusting it, it sounded like he said "self-help slut." Of course, it was nothing of that sort at all, but I knew at that moment that's what I would name the workbook series. The clients who I'd been working with for all these years had beautiful hearts, yet they lacked the belief that they were worthy of knowing or understanding anything of the spirit world. Many had been taught that only a select few are worthy of the spiritual walk. They were people who'd been discarded by their families or friends and made to feel as if they were worthless. I grew up feeling the same way—feeling that I could never be loved. Therefore, I believe this series can be helpful to everyone, male or female, who wishes to clear their energy field and raise their frequency through healing trauma and relationship contracts that they've carried in this life.

Many of you have read my first book, *How I Found My Superpowers*. If you haven't had the chance to yet, you might consider reading it as a foundation for the clearing work we are undertaking. It will introduce many of the ideas we'll build on as we move through this series.

There have been hundreds of spiritual books written, but many of them leave the reader feeling not good enough or ready for the spiritual endeavors the books talk about. In the channelings I've done, I've found no other publication that explains how, when, and why getting our spiritual origin reestablished is so important.

To start this workbook series, we'll take a deep look at the concept of the energy field and why it's the first place we need to concentrate our attention. Once you begin to clear the clutter there, other opportunities along your spiritual journey will begin to open. We'll focus on how you collect debris in your field and how it requires self-awareness to recognize what exactly you need to address. Once you learn how to clear your energy field of other people's shit, it will allow you to experience greater peace and accelerated personal growth.

The fact is that, depending on your interaction with others, there's more left in your energy field from them than you can imagine. That's right! We often walk around carrying debris from others' energy, actions, and behavior patterns—things that don't even belong to us.

This workbook series will help you clear your energy field and upgrade your template to the highest vibration by dispelling all the negative influences or self-sabotaging beliefs you've taken on. If you remember, in *How I Found My Superpowers*, I shared the story from my childhood of the Peeping Tom at the kitchen window when, though I was just age seven, my mother called me a slut. While I didn't even know the word or its meaning at the time, it was a term that she continued to use when she would get jealous. So, in a sense, if a person can get past the stigma imposed by society, family, or belief of a certain word or phrase like *slut*, then they are on the path to becoming their authentic self. And, they can begin clearing their energy field of other people's shit like I did with my mother.

The same formula that I'll be teaching you here is the one I've used in helping to clear relationship cords and trauma from my life and others'. Sometimes, things that you forgot about or thought of as insignificant may still reside in your energy field.

I urge you that while you're working through these workbooks, don't share any of what comes up with others. Please know that it's important to keep your secrets and your thoughts that you have written out private until the end of the course. I tell you this because there are several of you who are in relationships where, when you share something with the other person, they bring it up in an argument and use it as ammunition against you. This also occurs within families and sometimes between the closest connections. Your thoughts and your clearing process should not be used in that way. The pages that lie before you are a place for you to feel comfortable and to be able to open all that you've held within and all that you're ready to release.

While you're on your path, this workbook will allow you to work at your own pace—no one is pressuring you to complete it. The ideas have been laid out to guide you toward your highest and best outcome. I've added light and love to these pages with a high frequency. Once you begin clearing your energy field, you won't be able to stop. In my experience, when your higher self and spirit guides see your desire to be open to your true origin, it gives them greater power to help keep you on track. The process is not to be rushed, and as you move ahead, you can always go back and revisit the thoughts and feelings you shared on these pages. My hope for you is that as you purge through each step and each chakra, you can clear successfully. This will help you recognize any debris that you've collected at any moment through a relationship or encounter.

The first thing I need you to do as you work through this book is to begin to release all judgment that you've had toward yourself. I would like you to see yourself through a kinder lens. As you reflect on the exercises in the book, think of yourself as an objective outside observer would rather than being your own worst critic. I'll remind you of this periodically throughout the workbooks. I ask this of you to help you heal.

There will be several things that I'll ask you to gather while you're working through these pages so you'll be able to truly purge everything that needs to be released. Each workbook in this series will guide you through different levels while clearing each chakra. I ask that you hold on to each workbook until you've completed them all. This way, you have a reference point for how much work you've been able to do and how much you've been able to release. During this time, find a safe place to keep your workbooks until the course is completed. I would also ask you to date each page as you go along. I found it very helpful in my own studies and my own clearing to be able to go back and look at the date on each page and see the change in how I was feeling over time. Remember not to share your answers or experiences with anyone you are in a love relationship with for now. This will keep you from regretting that you exposed yourself during your purging process, as the experience or truths may be used as a weapon in the heat of anger.

If you've been watching my videos on TikTok, you know I'm all about grounding to settle your body down. Through grounding, things that need to be removed or revealed will come up.

We as humans travel from one experience to another day by day. Most of us have no idea why we have an interaction with someone else or what the higher purpose is for ourselves, the other person, or both. Most encounters happen for our greater good to help elevate our perception in reaching the spiritual understanding we came here for.

No matter how long you've been on your spiritual path, you may find there is always something more to purge. Throughout the book, I will share situations and things I've discovered in the energy fields of people in some of the most interesting career fields, along with my observations from those encounters. Throughout my books, the stories I share will encompass everything I've witnessed and researched in trying to understand the human experience during my lifetime.

I will also share some of the experiences from my past lives and what I learned from them.

The first thing I would like you to do is find a picture of yourself between the ages of zero and seven. You'll need this photo throughout this workbook and the entire series. Once you have it, you can use it as a bookmark as you move along in the book since you'll need to refer to it from time to time. If you don't have a baby or childhood photo available, that's fine. You may also want to have a photo of yourself from what you deem as the toughest time that you've experienced.

Please don't rush through the book. The journey will allow your being to move along at your own pace because your spiritual path is not a sprint—it's a marathon. As you work through the chapters, you may find yourself experiencing what is referred to as a healing crisis. This may show up as needing extra sleep or feeling tearful. If you find yourself going through these types of painful moments, recognize that they are signs you are moving through difficulty toward peace and that you'll feel better as your clearing progress continues. In the meantime, treat yourself with extra compassion and care.

After you finish this workbook and feel you've cleared and have moved beyond the experiences you had during the extractions of energies left behind by other people who had a direct influence on your life, there may still be things that come back to your memory for release. I would recommend you date the pages as you work. It will be helpful to be able to look back at your opinions so you can track the changes in your mindset and feelings later.

It has been my experience when working with others and releasing my own trauma that when we begin to clear, we recognize the fact that we are now safe and have made it through to forge a new life. Today is brand new and has never been experienced before, so let's make it the day we claim our power and reclaim the fragmented parts of our soul that we unknowingly gave away.

Chapter 1

The Releasing

Have you ever been around someone, and there seemed to be something off about them? Maybe you felt uneasy or repelled by their presence. In contrast, have you ever encountered someone you felt strongly drawn toward? Did you ever consider where these feelings came from? Could *they* have been having the same feeling about *you*? Well, those are great questions, and they can be answered with two words—*energy field*. Your personal energy field consists of the energy that flows in and around your body. And since EVERYTHING is energy and ENERGY is everything, our experience is affected by whatever comes in or near our energy field.

When our soul wants us to experience a lesson, even the most undesirable events can be the means of learning. We, as humans, clearly realize this, considering the abundance of books written about life lessons. We all carry a frequency in our energy field that acts as an energetic identification. This identifier is carried with us in every lifetime we experience. As we interact with one another, our energy field may be affected by the negative energy identifiers of other people, places, or things. The type of interaction will determine if the negative energy identifier becomes embedded in our energy field and, therefore, if it can create problems: physical, emotional, relational, and spiritual. An example is having an argument with another person while being in a depressive state. Because your frequency is in a lower state of vibration at this time, you'll be more susceptible to their negative energy identifiers. When this happens, you must learn how to clear that energy.

I would like you to envision a Little League baseball field. Now think about those tall chain-link fences on each side. Have you ever noticed how a chip bag or a plastic bottle gets picked up when the wind blows and pressed against the fence? The breeze can continue to blow through, but that piece of trash is unable to move. It becomes entangled in the wires and is stuck there until someone comes along and picks it up.

This is how our energy field operates daily—it will pick stuff up in the same way. When you're around others, no matter who they are, you're collecting debris in the most unsuspected ways. For example, the people you pass in the grocery store or at the park might unknowingly transfer energetic fragments to you. These items can become embedded in your field, and you may not realize that they need to be cleaned out since no major event such as a fight made you think twice about the casual outing.

How do you know when you may be carrying an array of debris? These are the times that your body feels heavy, tired, and sometimes depressed.

I didn't just wake up knowing this information. There were times when I felt overwhelmed by other people's energy. It wasn't until I began learning about the energy field that I began to ask those in the spirit world what was happening, and they explained that there are tethers, hooks, and some sort of an energy transfer to and from others' energy fields.

I began noticing different things in people's energy fields and didn't know what all those things meant. I soon learned that the dominant color surrounding a person's field was determined by the color of the portal their soul entered through when they incarnated. These different colored portals influence a soul's path during its lifetime on Earth. They are often referred to as the seven rays of light: blue, yellow, pink, red, green, orange, and purple. These are different from the colors that come up when perceiving emotions, illnesses, and experiences, which are often referred to as auric colors. There are also markings and objects that can be found in the energy field. It's obvious when items are embedded by being tied to the person's spiritual knowledge, but other objects look very odd and appear to be tied to experiences that are not so pleasant. An example is seeing a metal clamp around one's neck that had been placed there several lifetimes before. This could represent a trauma experienced by the person that has not been cleared.

The significance of each different marker in people's fields wasn't something that I sat around and pondered. I found it was much easier to discover what they indicated when people would talk about what they were experiencing or ask questions.

As they would phrase a question, I would hear the answer regardless of whether they were asking me or addressing someone else. So when people began to complain about their energy or how they were feeling, the answers would come up. Their spirit guides would show me something in their energy field and then explain what the event was attached to and what needed to be done to remove it. That was when I began to take notes. It seemed for everyone who came across my path, regardless of whether our encounter was personal or professional, I couldn't help but remember the information that I had accumulated. Then the knowledge was sorted into various topics. When I would encounter a new situation, my guides would show me which category it linked to and how it could bring a new understanding to the subject.

I began to compile information on just about every topic, from the body to past life adventures. This information became super important to me when I was reading with someone. As I would look at their energy field, my spirit guides would point things out and remind me of other situations that I'd seen previously. Sometimes, they would even say "remember," then say a person's name and tell me there was a correlation between what was happening with the current client and what had happened in a past reading I had done.

Things my spirit guides show me may not make sense to others, but they do to me. When your spirit guides begin to show you things, they'll highlight those lessons that will be clear to you. It's just like when you and a friend have an inside joke, and one word from the joke may not make sense to the rest of us, but it's funny to you. This is how you'll become familiar with what your guides want to show you. It may not always be something big; it can be a song they make sure you notice or a conversation you may only hear one word of.

I'd like to remind you, or share if you didn't know, that your spirit guides will never tell you to do anything mean to anyone else or to yourself. They are there to help you reach your highest purpose and the life path for which you came to incarnate.

Often, your spirit guides are people you knew during your in-between lives or during prior lifetimes. They love you, and their purpose is to roll out your blueprint every single day and see how much closer you are to reaching your goal. Your spirit guides are your most important allies next to God. The angels who volunteered to work with your spirit guides will continue to pave the path for you as you work on the things that you need to accomplish.

One example that I laugh about often is when I pray for a parking spot. I say this in the car: "Please bring me to a parking spot right up close." And immediately, one opens. The one thing you need to remember is that your spirit guides and angels need to hear your voice as if they're standing in the room with you. Only God and your higher self can hear your thoughts. This is because you are an aspect of God, and your higher self is the divine, awakened part of you. So when I say only God and your higher self can hear you, it's because they essentially are you, and you are them. When talking to spirit guides and angels, they reside in a dimension that interacts with you, but they need to hear your words. If you have deceased loved ones, they can't hear your thoughts; they must hear you speak out loud because they are not an aspect of your being. The deceased have lives between those on Earth. They are actively having an experience, so when you call their name, they need to hear to come to you. The deceased visit around special occasions, but they have a life and are doing things. As humans, we miss being able to see them and go places with them, but they are continuing their journey way beyond the familiar scope of mortal life.

As you go through this book, it may help to conceptualize your body as a great vessel or temple. Think of one of the most beautiful monuments that you've ever seen or one of the most beautiful houses that you've ever walked through. Think of your soul living inside that temple or house. Your soul needs it while you're living here on Earth so that you can continue your mission. Therefore, it's important to care for your body. Whatever sits in the energy field—including any debris that you picked up during the day while you were out and engaging with people—will need to be cleared. When debris stays in our energy field for too long, it can cause issues within our physical body. Some of the residue that we pick up from relationships with other people can cause disease within the body. That debris, coupled with the thoughts that we had while interacting with those individuals, accounts for 70 percent of all diseases. The other 30 percent is from things that were gifted to us from our ancestors and relationships prior to age five. Whatever emotions, trauma, or energy you have taken on sits in your energy field, and when it's not worked through and cleared or released totally, it will move into the physical body.

To move forward through the workbook series with book two, we'll need to start with a clean slate. The clean slate I'm referring to is your energy field. This will allow any healing and acknowledgment of things or memories that we'd like to clear and purify to be seen as they should be and released in a proper way.

The fact that you're working through this workbook now is a sure sign that you're walking your spiritual path and want to continue to clear. Don't feel that you need to rush through these exercises. Please take your time to write on the pages and make notes. Don't leave anything out. If you're worried about someone else reading these items after you finish the book, you can tear out those pages and burn them or just tear them into tiny pieces and ask your angels to take them to the light. The words on the pages and the clearing that happens will be finalized in the ethers. Later, I'll explain more about the ethers and how your angels work together to help you achieve your highest and best.

When we experience abuse of any kind, whether verbal, physical, or mental, it tends to stay with us in our energy field until we clear it. This is the case even in situations where we feel like we've moved beyond it and have chalked it up to that person's way of being. Sometimes, our cellular bodies absorb part of the abuse and tuck it deep within.

There's no way of knowing when or why our bodies will do this, but sometimes we'll see the emotions come out later in other ways. The ways that I'm referring to are usually common experiences, but most people don't understand exactly why they happen. One example is tears coming out in periods of release during a movie. Think of a time you were watching a movie, and you didn't know why you started crying. Perhaps at the end of the story, you began to tear up, not understanding exactly why you were emotional.

You may not have had a reference point to reflect on in your own life that made you cry during the movie. Those emotions are often attached to prior situations from past lives.

The process of starting with a clean slate can be the best way to look at what needs to be released with honest eyes. When you are working through this book, you may recall a situation that, at the time, might not have felt like abuse because you chose to see it in another way or in a passive-aggressive way, and you felt you moved beyond it. Those moments leave remnants of debris that need to be dislodged from our fields. These often show up as energetic cords attached to the body, which we will discuss later in the chapter. (See Figure 1 for a glimpse of how it looks in the energy field when left uncleared.)

When you're working with any of the workbooks in this series, it's important to do so in an environment where you won't be disturbed. If you have no options other than a room with other people, that will have to do. Don't work in the workbook at times when you feel hurried, as it's important to begin allowing your inner voice to connect with your desires and thoughts. If you have feelings of anger that come up during the process of clearing, please take yourself outside to clear and reset your mind. If the weather permits a walk, that's the next best thing to grounding—a technique I'll explain in the next section. I've had trouble getting some clients to

Katharine Branham

ground when they have been upset, so I have them walk for a bit, then I help them ground.

28

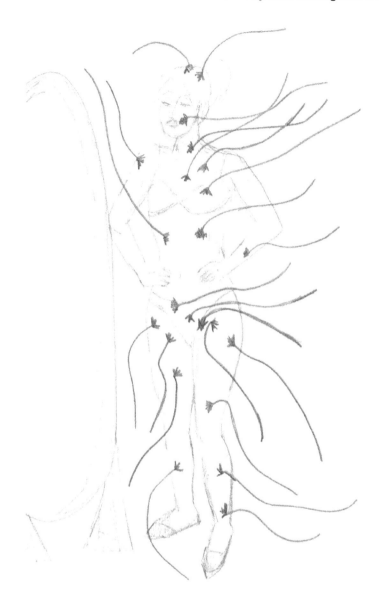

Figure 1—Uncleared cords attached in the energy field that you can't see in the mirror.

Grounding 101

Grounding is a technique to anchor to Mother Earth that will allow you to recalibrate your energy field and restore balance. It's always a good idea to start by centering yourself with a prayer that you say aloud. It can be something you feel guided to say, or you can simply ask your spirit guides to come in and help you.

This can be done standing or sitting in a chair. I prefer sitting. The time to ground standing is in situations when you need to calm yourself, such as in a hall before going into a class, a doctor's visit, the DMV, or another stressful situation that calls for a quick fix to anchor you. Otherwise, standing to ground is not recommended until you have a grasp of grounding in general. Also, when I've watched others try to ground while sitting on their bottom on the ground, I've noticed the energy doesn't flow as well. Therefore, a chair is the best option.

When you sit in a chair to begin grounding, see yourself as an Egyptian pharaoh or Egyptian queen—they knew how to harness energy. Those depictions we see of them sitting tall is so much more than an immortalizing pose. It's how they anchored their feet to the Earth and allowed the energy to flow. This energy is what would aid them in maintaining power, so to speak.

As we get into grounding, it's important to note that you can do this indoors or outdoors, although I prefer the outdoor environment. Follow the steps below:

Step 1 On your first attempt to ground, I would ask you to find your most comfortable chair. It needs to be one that when you sit, your feet can rest on the floor, not dangle. You should consider an appropriate comfort level in the area you choose to ground regarding light, sound, and temperature. Close your eyes, place your hands on top of your thighs, and breath naturally. You will not cross your legs, as you want the energy to flow smoothly. (See Figure 2.)

Step 2 When you're comfortable, you can begin to allow all the weight and heaviness from the top of your body to drop down to the lower part. You may want to see your energy at the top portion of your body as syrup. It's thick and moves slowly, but eventually, it all comes down as we allow gravity to do its part without restrictions. This takes a bit of time, so don't rush. As the energy or syrup makes its way to your feet, you will allow it to stream through the soles in the way a root grows off a tree. The idea is to envision roots from your feet growing deep into the Earth. As your roots begin to deepen, see them growing through the Earth's layers, such as the soil, rocks, and crystal kingdom, to the core of Mother Earth.

Step 3 Once you get to the core, keeping your eyes closed, you should rest in that connection for at least fifteen minutes.

I would like to mention that you can utilize crystals while grounding. This may help to enhance your experience, but it isn't necessary. Simply holding the crystal in your hand is the only technique you need to know at this level. A few of the best crystals worth mentioning for grounding are black tourmaline and any type of obsidian crystal. When you begin to master grounding, you'll be able to bring in your spirit guides for messages and direction. While in this state, there will also be times that messages will come to you even when you're not seeking them.

Figure 2—Sitting position for grounding. Focus on comfort.

When I spoke to Mother Mary, she told me that grounding was practiced during the time she walked the Earth. The ones among the population at that time who could see the energy field around their bodies and others' weren't special—it was normal.

Mother Mary continued to explain that the Earth contains ley lines, which are electrical currents that all living things move to and live by. This is also what ocean life follows and what energy travels by around the world. These ley lines are conduits for God source energy, which connect across the globe—offering restoration to the energy fields of all living organisms that seek realignment.

Often, when I tell someone to practice grounding, they look at me as if nothing could be that easy. You need to know that it is, and that's the way it's supposed to be. It was humanity who began to be complicated. Humanity has been pulled away from the source by outside travelers who visited our planet to mess with us.

Even when we are outdoors playing Frisbee or walking our dog, it gives us some connection to the Earth—though not to the extent that grounding does. Therefore, when I know I can't get someone to ground, I at least try to get them outside.

Mother Mary also taught me there was a time in history when every home had a garden of some sort that provided the interaction with the Earth that people needed. When certain cultures began to rely on grocery stores for all their food, they gave up their personal gardens, and that led to people staying indoors, not knowing that this pulled them away from their Earth connection. When this began to happen, depression among the population grew instead of gardens. The Earth is so important for living beings to balance their bodies.

There are now farmers in certain parts of the world who keep cows indoors, their whole existence connected to milking machines, while they watch artificial outdoor scenes designed to trick the animals. They never feel what real dirt is like under their hooves until they can no longer produce milk. Then cows are physically kicked out or lifted by a crane and loaded on a truck to the slaughterhouse for human consumption. The animals that are deformed or riddled with cancer are allowed to live in pain and suffering since the meat industry sees treatment as costly and allows the animals to shiver or shake in long deaths. Although not legally allowed in the US as far I know, in some places, that diseased animal is not discarded since its body is seen as a product—the animal is placed in the food system and is consumed by humans. When someone puts another being through that type of life, that person will feel all the sadness of their nightmarish existence ten times over at the time of their exit from the world. If the soul doesn't learn from that, it will reincarnate and have a life of that same treatment. (It is worth noting that the United States Department of Agriculture now has inspections in place aimed to prevent animals with cancer and certain other diseases from entering the food chain, and there are legal repercussions for those caught trying to bypass them.)

Most of humanity has no idea about the sadness and abuse cows, chickens, and other commercial farm animals are put through. The fact is that most of the population has no idea why they eat eggs for breakfast—it's just what has been done for generations. There's the phrase that we've all heard: "You are what you eat." If you eat sadness and death, you will feel every bit of that in your mind, body, and soul. When someone is feeling depressed, they look at their life, their partner, and their job, but they rarely look at the shit they eat.

Your soul is smart and knows so much more than you remember after passing through the veil of the Earth's atmosphere into mortal life.

You buy your ticket to Earth only after you've gone through a boot camp of rigorous spiritual training so you can achieve all you set out to do on your mission to make your life a success. So why is it a challenge to remember those lessons?

Did you ever use flashcards to help you in school? You would look at the card and try to remember the answer, then you would flip it over to see if you got it right. When you come to Earth, your flashcards are taken away, and you must dig deep to truly remember what the answer on the back was. It works this way so that your soul begins to hold steady with the embedded teachings until nothing else is even fathomable. That is when your soul hits a point during an incarnation that it reverts to its original blueprint of true north. True north is the setting of our origin from the creator, and that's what we are striving for when we begin to unveil our journey. It starts with grounding, enjoying the outdoors—providing the weather is good—and being kind to animals.

During the period that otherworldly beings visited the first groups of humans on Earth, certain practices were introduced. This led the population to shut down their individual spiritual antennas and follow those beings who seemed to be more powerful. It's through the clearing of this misconception that we will begin to restore our original blueprint.

Remember as you're clearing that if you get triggered, grounding or walking to reset will help you to get through the purging. If you like working out, I also suggest moving some weight if you feel guided to. When watching other people exercise, as I look around the gym, I can see how their unwanted energy is getting squeezed out. These people have no idea that they're clearing some crap from the energy field—though perhaps not all of it—when they work out. For example, a girl someone slept with two weeks ago may have imprinted an unwanted souvenir in his energy field, and through working out, it may have cleared a bit. He just knows he feels better.

The lists I have you make in each chapter throughout the workbook are very important in your release of energy associated with negative emotions, even if you think they don't matter. I suggest you date your lists and date any changes you make when you reread the workbook, whether two weeks from now or two years from now. As you move through your spiritual path, your higher frequency will show you the difference in your emotions at this very moment and the emotions you'll experience with your new spiritual eyes.

I would like you to think about the people who were in your life when you were between the ages of zero and five. This is important to the process. Please keep in mind any relatives you visited during this period. I would like you to keep the opinion you formed about them at that time in your life separate from the one you have now. Most people don't have a memory before age three, so please use what you felt when you would hear others talk about them.

You may find a deeper understanding of why a parent or grandparent told you something. Often, it was only their opinion based on their feelings of inadequacy that they were trying to cover because of their own guilt or shame.

Example from my life

When I was three years of age, I remember an argument my parents had. I was playing with dolls in my room and could hear Mom yelling at Dad. He was asking if she would like to drive up and see his mom, who was my Grammy. Mom declared that if he wanted to see her, he could drive over on his own while she visited with her mother, who only lived twenty minutes away.

In her desperate attempt to distract people from discovering anything about her father, she would draw attention away from him by making ugly remarks about others. It could be something small, like commenting on how Grammy's dog was yappy, to something bigger, like saying Grammy lived very poorly, not having air conditioning.

Dad seemed to feel bad about the way Grammy lived in contrast to Mom's parents, so he said, "Grammy would still like to see the kids." When I walked into the kitchen, I told Mom I would like to go see my Grammy. She looked at me and said, "You have no idea how she lives, and you wouldn't like the dog." I stood there thinking about Grammy's dog. It was a wiener dog, and while it was yappy, it was the only family Grammy had at home.

My father had lost his dad at the age of seventeen. My grandfather had come from Greece and opened restaurants and diners in New York and Maine before moving to Texas. When he died, my Grammy sold the business since she didn't feel she could run it on her own. She mourned tremendously for him, as he was her true love and they had a bond that could be felt by anyone who knew them.

Meanwhile, Mom found additional ways to try and discredit others to make her feel better about her experiences. She claimed that people who owned clubs or diners were wild. She would often say how her parents were decent people, and her dad never ran around on her mom and would bring his paycheck home, alluding to the fact many men would drink and squander money while their family suffered. I didn't know what that meant at the time and didn't realize she'd been trying to cover the guilt she felt from her father's abuse.

The truth was that my father's parents weren't uncouth or dishonorable. It was the only way she found to prevent others from knowing or realizing the truth of her own situation—by either shaming them or telling the past as she would like it to be seen. People often do this when the guilt is deep; they divert the finger-pointing and name-calling onto others.

This experience was and still is a common practice that takes place in many families—many children are made to feel bad about things that have happened to them rather than looking at the person who was the abuser, which in my mom's case was her father. Mom denied all hurt and scared feelings by attacking others she thought might see through her. There's often jealousy involved. Mom needed to be the center of Dad's attention, and when he would visit Grammy, the attention went to her. Mom would keep the visits short and rush us out.

You can see by the story above that when we are children, the adults around us sometimes make comments based on their judgment and fears. When you are digging deep into how you felt about a person you knew or still know, separate off the opinions of other adults during the time period in question. By just sticking to the time period, you will have memories come up that will clear as we go through this together.

Exercise #1

Now let's do an exercise to identify the people in your life who have impacted your energy field:

Step 1 Please take a moment and list the people below who were in your life between the ages of zero and five. Next to their names, write the connection they had to you (i.e., mom, dad, aunt, family friend). Include those who might have just been around during that time, even if you felt you had very little interaction with them.

Step 2 Write down any feelings or memories that may come up. Sometimes, as you begin to allow the energy connected to a certain situation to release or, at the very least, come to the surface, more memories will arise.

Step 3 Now I would like you to think about the traits of these people. Please close your eyes, lean back, and think of each individual you listed. What is one main characteristic that you remember about this person? (When you're doing this step, don't think about what your mom thought of them; this is *your* opinion at that time. The feelings should be only how you felt about them. Did you trust them? Remember, you only need to think about what you knew of them at that time, not in later years.)

*If you can't remember much about a person, just take the impression you get when you think about them. Was the memory negative or positive? You can put an **N** for negative and **P** for positive. Please keep in mind this is between ages zero and five.

(Example: Ann Stern—family friend who visited us almost every day

I was 4 years old

She would sit outside, drink wine, and make fun of my friends and me

Negative: I felt worthless, inferior, hurt. I was often scared that she would hit me)

1)_____

_____

_____

_____

_____

_____

2)_____

_____

_____

_____

_____

_____

3)_____

_____

_____

_____

_____

_____

4)_____

_____

_____

_____

Katharine Branham

5)

6)

7)

8)_____

_____

_____

_____

_____

_____

9)_____

_____

_____

_____

_____

_____

10)_____

_____

_____

_____

_____

_____

If you've heard me talk about cleaning cords as opposed to just cutting them, you probably have a good handle on the concept. The practice of cutting cords doesn't clean or remove them properly. To merely cut them will always leave you with the haunting feelings that developed with the individuals and the memories embedded with emotions. This means the abuse and trauma you may have taken on will continue to circulate in a boomerang fashion until they're handled properly. The cord is the first thing we will begin to clear.

Now refer back to the list that we just made of those in your early years of life. These are the key people who either lifted you up or weighed you down with emotions that weren't yours. If there's no one on your list who you felt you had a negative experience with, then look at an experience you wish would have been better. The ones you have a negative memory of will be the people you will clean the cords with first.

You will go one by one, starting at the top of your list and going down to clean the negative cords. If one of the people was a parent or guardian and you still interact with the person, this will help you not to feel the heaviness of the connection by helping you disconnect from the emotions of the troubled times.

Cord Cleaning 101

*Make sure you mark this page for easy reference, as you'll be referred back here throughout the workbook.

Cord cleaning only works when you're truly ready to release. If you still find yourself in victim mode—even the slightest bit— you'll need to repeat the process a few times. Please know that even if this person is deceased, it needs to be done so there's no carryover in their next life.

Step 1 You will begin by holding the image of the person in your mind's eye. If you're having difficulty doing this, then I ask you to grab a picture, and if that's not an option, write the person's full name along with any nicknames they used.

Step 2 Please only say this next part when you're ready. If you read through it and feel it's not your truth, come back to the exercise at a time when you feel more prepared.

While seeing the person in your mind or looking at the photo, you will say:

"Thank you for the experience of our connection. I've learned all I wish to from you—I'm grateful for the place I'm at on my journey, and I no longer need the emotional pain or physical pain that was taken on by our exchange. I release it with love and light to the Universe for transmutation and purification."

Step 3 While holding the thought of love and peace in your heart, use your intuition to visualize where the cord is on your body. Go with the first thought that comes to you. Visualize this cord like a garden hose coming out of your body. Use your hand and grab the hose where it is coming out of your body. Gently stroke it with your other hand in an outwardly motion as though you are cleaning mud off your garden hose. It may take a while, so don't rush. Once it's clear, grasp it from the base of the cord and pull it out completely. This will have the feel of pulling a carrot from the ground. You can allow the end of the cord to be released to the light of the Universe. This is a great visual for you to feel and see. Don't worry about pulling out the root attached to the other person. I would suggest visualizing a clean, sparkling color at the spot where the cord had been attached. When I'm doing this exercise, I will choose the first color that comes to mind since I know that's the color my intuition feels is needed for the spot. I add sparkles so it's extra clean in my mind.

I should tell you that if you're still in victim mode and are not ready to clean the cord for release when you try this, the feeling and thoughts of the person will continue to come up. Therefore, if the process needs to be repeated, don't get upset with yourself. The practice will remove emotional layers that will start the foundation for you to be totally free of that connection. On the other hand, if you do this process with the readiness to clear and move forward, you will feel a light feeling in the next few days, which is always a great indicator that you're cleared. You can return to this section as needed while you move along in the book.

Even after all the clearing I've done within my own energy field, some things still come to the surface that weren't ready to be released until I budged on other obstacles. Those obstacles could be a mindset or a false memory of how I perceived the experience at the time of a trauma. They may also include new information that is finally understood when hidden truths are revealed to make sense of an experience where I had a different perspective at the time of the incident.

The people you may feel you need to clean a cord to might be a short list now, but as you move through this book, the list will grow. As you begin to clear, more memories will surface and become ready for healing. I like to teach with stories so you can allow the information to sink in and so the things you are ready to release can come up. As you continue the process, memories may begin to make sense to you, and you may be able to see others' viewpoints at the time of the situation. Please don't judge yourself; just let it flow when you're ready. There's no rush or judgment in the spirit world, so if something takes a little longer to clear, see the timing as perfect.

Chapter 2

The Filters

There are some filters humanity collectively and unconsciously chooses to look through. Some of these filters are worn in the energy field. Individually, whether a person is affected by a filter depends upon their ability to separate what is reality and what is perception of the ego. The filters that I'm referring to are ideas the mind holds from societal or cultural misguidance. If we allow these ideas to become our truth without using our inner spiritual guidance to feel out the information, then it becomes filtered. We are usually surprised when we later find out the truth in its unfiltered state.

Many situations are shown in ways that help us learn the difference between the things humanity teaches each other out of ego and things that are spiritual knowledge, though neither of these should be perceived as good or bad. Do you know of a person who might have identified with one belief only later to see the fractures in what they thought was a great way to live? This often happens when a person is able to shift their understanding and remove a filter. When we begin to walk our spiritual path, it can help us start to make these shifts for ourselves.

There are souls who come into this life with filters already in place. Some people choose to place a filter on who they are. This is the soul's way to protect itself and avoid repeating a miserable experience it had in the past. If a person admired a certain individual in a past life, they often strive to live like that person during this life. Some choose to identify as someone from our history they perceive as great. The memory of that famous person often lingers from either watching a movie or reading a book. They begin to see themselves as the famous person they loved in another lifetime. I learned this lesson after nearly a thousand different people asked me if they were Cleopatra. It was shown to me spiritually that these men, women, and children who thought they were Cleopatra in a past life had fallen in love with the idea from history books or the movie version of Cleopatra, played by Elizabeth Taylor. The history of humanity has glamorized and left out so much that people don't know how to separate what has been taught by ego and what is truth. If humanity really knew what Cleopatra was about, no one would want to claim to be her.

There have been books written about people's experiences with past life regression, a form of hypnotherapy that helps individuals access memories from previous lifetimes, and what the findings of the sessions have been. Even Dolores Cannon, who spent her whole life studying hypnosis with a wide variety of people, found very few who had previously been someone famous. Many people get confused because once you cross to the other side, you're able to go to the Akashic records and view any lifetime or any period that you've ever wanted to see. In fact, it doesn't have to be a lifetime that *you* experienced. It's like going into a library where you can check out any book you want and partake in the experiences of the author through reading their story, even though the experiences weren't yours to begin with. It's a wonderful learning opportunity, but sometimes when memories of those tales are brought to the surface, people can mistake the things they've read or viewed for events they experienced in a past life.

The only time important past lives come up is when a person is carrying trauma from that life that needs to be overcome or cleared. This means that the outcome or the situation tied to the trauma continues to repeat. There is usually a filter that will only dissolve once it's ready to clear, either because the individual faced the truth in acceptance or worked on self-awareness. Filters may come up at times when you experience similar situations and you're triggered by the fear that the trauma or experience will happen again. One similar lesson in each lifetime may come up until you finally decide to break the loop. Many people don't understand they're stuck in a loop with a filter that needs to be cleared, nor do they understand how to break it.

When you're in a karmic loop, you continue to experience a similar situation, unable to move beyond it through a series of lifetimes. Your higher self, your spirit guides, and your angels are guiding you. To break the loop means choosing a higher outcome than you've chosen before. Hypnosis can help in clearing the fragmented soul from trauma when you're ready. It's crucial that when we hit a point in our life where it may become difficult, we push forward and exhaust every avenue in trying to fix our situation. Clearing, releasing energy work, or hypnosis all work great at moving the energy, allowing the release to happen—or at least begin.

I've found that most people don't know how to ask for help. This stems from long-held familial beliefs that asking for help is shameful. This is something that needs to be removed from our templates. Asking for help is not shameful—in fact, it's one of the most honorable things you can do when you look at what it takes to get here on Earth and how long it takes to get through childhood situations attached to family. I would like you to see it as you would when you're riding with someone in the car and they don't want to stop and ask for directions. For whatever reason, they're bent on trying to figure out the route on their own—as if stopping for directions would show that they're incompetent. This is far from the truth when you're dealing with your life. If you stop to ask for help when difficult moments come up, someone else can guide you until you finally find your route out of your difficult time. Sometimes, stopping to ask for help from another source can lead you to a beautiful experience and perhaps one that had been set up for you all along. When the family dynamic has been imprinted as being secretive or guilt-ridden, many feel they can't turn to their family, as their family may not accept their decision or even be open to it.

The reality is that a low percentage of people in the world are born into a family that completely accepts who they are and what they're here to accomplish. Actor Matt Dillon is a great example of one who was able to find his path. He was discovered by Jane Bernstein and a friend while he was skipping class. At the time, Jane was helping Jonathan Kaplan cast for a violent teen drama called *Over the Edge*. This was the step that led Matt to his life mission and the experience he needed. Matt was one of six children from a very strict Catholic household. Just looking at his situation prior to his success in acting, you might have thought there wasn't a chance the young man would be given an opportunity to be an actor. You can see by Matt's example the Universe made a way for him. There are thousands of stories just like this in various life situations. So it doesn't really matter which family you're born into or the location in which you live—when something is meant to be, the Universe will bring it in for you and drop it along your path so you're unable to miss it. When you come across an opportunity like that, it's very important to tune in.

During the year 2015, I noticed more people opening to their spiritual paths. The ones who were avoiding their eyes being opened were pushed onto their spiritual path through one situation or another. Some things just had to happen, and sometimes those things weren't pleasant, but they were necessary to force souls to find their way. I've spoken to thousands of people who had to lose someone to start walking their spiritual path or to even consider thinking about the other side and realizing that something exists there. As you may know if you've watched some of the videos that I've posted, you're never alone; the spirit world is always with you and is assisting you in finding what you came here for.

When you incarnate into a fresh life, your cellular memory begins recording on day one. This happens even if nothing noteworthy is happening. Your cells record data just like a computer. For experiences that are traumatic, cells will hold on to the data even when the cell rebuilds, clears, or renews. The information continues to be stored. That's why sometimes it takes years to release trauma. I've been at the point where I thought, *Okay, surely it's all been released by now*, only to find out there were still threads that I was unable to look at. These threads are often connected to a specific situation, time, geographical location, or even shame.

Humans begin creating shame for babies from day one. It sometimes begins as a comment from the parents about how the baby was conceived, then it moves on to an undesirable physical characteristic taken on from one side of the family or another. This commentary begins to happen before the infant can start forming his or her own opinions. So as the infant lies there cooing, it has already taken others' feelings about the situation surrounding its conception and now has to deal with judgments on appearance. This only continues to pile up as the child gets older. This is emotional karma transferred by family members. Now let's add any emotional or mental imbalances that parents, grandparents, or other family members are going through. This occurs because the baby doesn't have any chakra filters in place to protect it from the negative energies—words, actions, or influences—in its environment. This is why childhood trauma is so difficult to clear—because it's so deeply rooted in the energy field.

The perceptions of everyone else in the family are taken on, and sometimes as we grow, we are made to feel this is our own fault. This is the number one reason we must clear our energy field and pay attention to anything else that begins to surface along our path. The human energy field is complex, with layers of emotions that get packed in, and before you know it, you're carrying around more than you can manage.

As humanity evolved, we got further away from the daily cleansing process we had naturally practiced. These practices were only in place for less than a hundred years before the practices were discarded by rulers and early religious rituals. The practices of clearing, centering, and grounding were discouraged, so humanity couldn't feel what they needed to and began to follow the guidance of what came to be understood as control. The clearing process will help to release the very fibers that have carried through the bloodlines and teachings you've been trained to believe. As these old emotions and memories surface to clear, you'll notice a difference in your energy. It will feel like chains and shackles being removed from your being.

As more and more religions formed, so did the misdirection of man's steps. This misdirection pulled us further from the creator until we found ourselves resembling only by mere physical appearance that which we once were when the creator brought us here. Most of the planet is operating on the autopilot of failed human efforts and not the original blueprint of our true spiritual essence.

Exercise #2

Now I'd like you to make a list of people you feel are opposed to your beliefs or the way you live. It's important to take your time and include a few reasons that indicate why they don't accept who you are or your beliefs. These lists are for you to look back at and have an *ah-ha* moment as you reflect on the mentality behind their inability to honor your choices or decisions.

(Example: Aunt Truly—I was divorced and stopped attending church to follow my spiritual path)

1)

_____

_____

2)

_____

_____

3)

_____

_____

4)

_____

_____

5)

_____

_____

6)

_____

_____

7)

_____

_____

As you begin to clear, you may have physical experiences and sensations that change, such as developing a dislike for certain fabrics and textures of clothing on your skin. The most common way of knowing you're clearing is when you are in your old normal setting, and it feels like you don't belong. For example, you may be engaging in conversation about hobbies or activities that once brought you joy, and there will be a disconnect or the feeling, _What am I doing here? This is no longer fun._

This will be the time when your frequency is on the rise and you no longer wish to relish in some of your old three-dimensional ways of coping, such as alcohol, drugs, smoking, or eating anything with a soul. These three-dimensional ways I mention are all things that keep a soul from reaching its original blueprint of self. It keeps the soul tethered to humanity by a type of karma, like death with pain. Many people have no idea, but when we hand a friend a glass of wine, we've tethered them to the ground of the third dimension, no matter how much we say we love them. We do it to ourselves when we drink wine. It's not the intention at the time of consumption—it's the origin of those items and the thought behind why they were produced, given, made, and abused. It's the torment they've caused that still echoes in the world today. When you research the history of alcohol itself, it has always been used with manipulation. Many of the vineyards all over the world used slave labor, and when some did offer payment, the owners paid in wine to enslave people to the addiction. It has been used in war, to impregnate, and to enslave. The threads of alcohol are man-made, and it's a souvenir that many don't know they carry.

When the soul reincarnates into every life, there are troubling aspects of our past earthly behavior that we carry in our field until they're cleared. The threads of alcohol are in the energy field of tiny babies until they're cleared. The threads can be from the lineage of the soul family tethered to alcoholism or from a past life that they have come here to clear. The clearing can happen on an unconscious level if you experience a similar situation in the new life and you choose not to participate, coming to see that there's a better way. Alternately, you can clear it through the spiritual understanding that the previous behavior is not the best for you when offered to partake. It can also occur on a physical level by removal with surgery on the body or even dental issues. It will depend on what threads you carry from the event or belief it was linked to. Therefore, the cords are not always connected to the liver, which is the organ most notably affected by alcohol.

Exercise #3

Take some time now and consider the people or places that come to mind when you think about alcohol. Also, write the emotion you feel when you think of the person or place and a word associated with the thought of alcohol. Do you think the people on the list were truly happy people?

(Example: My neighbor Anne—smelled like alcohol, always seemed angry)

1)

_____

_____

2)

_____

_____

3)

_____

_____

4)

_____

_____

5)

_____

_____

6)

_____

_____

7)

_____

_____

When I was in high school, I attended a party with my friend Michelle. It was the event that people had talked about for weeks, so you can imagine that it was a large gathering. She lived in the same neighborhood where the party was happening, so we walked over. When we arrived, there looked to be at least one hundred people in attendance. Michelle wanted to run into this guy she liked, who had told her he would be there. When I reached the driveway, I had a weird feeling about the party. I knew I wasn't in danger, but I felt I would somehow be learning a lesson. I felt the frequency telling me I was safe. Michelle and I had picked up sub sandwiches earlier, and I had half of my sub and a bag of chips left. I thought once Michelle saw her guy, we would leave.

There was a large pool around back, where a few couples were making out. I found a chaise lounge and opened my sandwich. I'd only been sitting there for fifteen minutes when a guy named Marcus walked up and sat down. I could tell he liked me when he would talk to me at school. He was five-ten and had piercing light-brown eyes, which stood out much more against the dark canvas of his skin. It felt as if he could stare right through a person when he looked at them. I could tell when a guy in biology class chased me with a frog part how Marcus's energy field went into protector mode as he jumped in front of me, staring the guy down. He worked at Taco Bell and often brought me a treat after his shift.

"So the party has been going on for two hours, and the pool still looks clean," I said while wondering if he came with anyone.

"Yes, I noticed that. Do you want to swim?" he said, suggesting we jump in as he turned his head the other way—possibly to keep me from noticing his smile.

"Maybe later," I answered. "Want a bite of my sandwich and chips?"

He took a chip, then offered to go in and get us something to drink. When he returned with the drinks, he was proudly holding up two Sunkist sodas. "There's so much beer in there. Cases and kegs, then two huge coolers: one with Mountain Dew and the other Sunkist. I know how much you love Sunkist, so I got us each one." He was looking into my eyes while he popped open the can.

I was relieved he wasn't a drinker, noticing there were no threads of alcohol in his field. "So, how long have you been here?" I asked while wondering if he had made out with anyone before I got there. He didn't seem like the type of guy who would make out with someone, then ignore them for the rest of the night.

He shook his head, and as he did, an image of a girl was trying to release from his energy field. The image wasn't connected to his heart. As he began to talk, he took longer than normal to get his words out. He explained that some girl who had a reputation of being promiscuous was in one of the bedrooms randomly having sex. I could tell by his energy field he was sad for her. He exclaimed, "She's does this quite often from what I've heard."

Then I noticed a cord from him to her, so I asked, "Do you know the girl?"

"No, not really. I've seen her at school, but she's not my type, and I've heard she sleeps with anyone. I just didn't imagine her doing something like this."

I needed to pee, so he offered to walk me in and stand by the door. I felt it was his way of being protective since the house was crowded. When we walked in, there was a group at the kitchen table playing quarters. Quarters was a drinking game where there were a few people sitting around the table, and they could either bounce the quarter off the table into the cup of beer or they could roll it off their nose. If they missed the cup, they'd drink. Michelle was sitting at the table with the guy she liked while he played. I motioned to her that I had Marcus's hand as he was guiding me down the hall.

Marcus had a beautiful golden energy field. I didn't know what the golden field meant at the time, but I knew it was special. I later learned that those with the golden field were unstoppable, and they came with a very rare mission to Earth as they embodied precious love that was patient and unconditional. He played football, made good grades, and seemed to have his priorities in order.

He led me through the crowd and opened the bathroom door, telling me he would wait there. The music was loud, and as I was exiting the bathroom, a guy named Sam was talking to Marcus. They quickly stopped when I opened the door. The guy talking to him had dark-gray energy around the edges of his auric field with a gray-green color at the midsection of his body and groin. When we made it through the crowd and back to the lounge by the pool, a spiritual cord I'd noticed earlier that was attached to Marcus was more prominent than before.

"So, what did that guy want outside the bathroom?" I asked while still holding his hand.

He looked up, and his eyes seemed more piercing than before. "He wanted to know if I had any condoms. Sam told me no one has any more condoms, so the guys in line to be with the girl in the bedroom are going to use plastic sandwich bags."

As I sat there listening to Marcus, I was guided to think back to Sam's energy field and was shown that it was a sexually transmitted disease discoloration that I had seen. It seemed the whole thing was bothering Marcus, and the cord attached to him made me wonder if he liked the girl in the room. The frequency of God came through and conveyed that Marcus wasn't attracted to her at all and had no affection for her other than care for her well-being. It told me to be patient as he worked through the process. My human perception was that of a fourteen-year-old who was viewing the situation from a very small perspective.

Marcus then began to explain that he couldn't imagine why she was okay with sleeping with all those guys. He also told me he only came to the party because he knew I was going to be there. I noticed a filter of some sort in Marcus's heart. The filter was there as a protection of the belief he held from a rejection he had faced. He was extremely good-looking, so his facing rejection seemed so doubtful. Michelle came out about that time and said she was ready to go, so Marcus walked us both home.

The following Monday, Marcus stopped by my locker. He asked if I could meet him at the bleachers outside for lunch. The school was abuzz with talk about the party. The bedroom girl was a no-show at school. When I met up with Marcus, he pulled his lunch out, looking carefully at the contents. I could tell he wanted to express something to me, but he was hesitant. He avoided eye contact as he told me that he had been adopted and his mom had told him the name of his biological mother. As he was speaking, I noticed a clearing from his energy field that indicated that the potential of meeting his biological mother might provide a purge of something major. It looked the way the wind felt before a major storm when you could sense the shift of energy in the air.

A few days went by with very little chance to talk to Marcus. One afternoon, he came by Michelle's, where I'd been staying after school, and he wanted to talk. We sat on the driveway, and he began to tear up while trying to look away. "I got the address to my birth mom's house, and I went over there," he said while still glancing off. "I knocked on the door, and when it opened, it was the girl from the bedroom." He sat there in silence for a moment before continuing. "The girl opened the door and said, 'What are you here for?' I told her I was looking for Doris King." His head turned farther away, preventing me from being able to see his eyes. "I asked if Ms. King lived there. The girl said Doris was her mom, then opened the door all the way so I could see a woman who was half-dressed, sprawled out on an old recliner. The woman didn't even get up from the chair. She just said, 'Yeah, who are you?' I told her I was the boy she gave up, and I just wanted to see what she looked like. She said, 'Okay, so now you've seen what I look like. I had too much to drink the night I became pregnant with you.'"

As Marcus was explaining this to me, I could see that the thread to the bedroom girl was only through their biological connection. The interaction with the birth mother severed the thread for good. He felt no connection to the woman who brought him into the world. He went on to tell me how much he loved the mother who raised him, Maxine, and after meeting Doris, he would never question his true mother. There seemed to be a calm that came over him. The filter that was in his heart chakra that had previously been a block was now gone. Marcus and I hung out from time to time until he left for college. At a graduation party his parents threw for him, there was a visible cord I could see connected from him to Maxine, his dad James, and Shantel, the sister he was raised with. Maxine and James adopted both Marcus and Shantel, but the heart cords of love were there as if they were blood.

It doesn't matter who chooses to be your mom after you're born; it's the true cords of love that define the soul connections that are meant to be. I came to understand filters that are placed in certain chakras by experiences or protection are there to allow the spiritual growth that needs to take place before they are dissolved. Not everyone who has had a similar experience with a biological family member accepts why the filters are there. In Marcus's case, it was so he could be the person he came to be and be free of the karmic loop that Doris and her daughter were stuck in together. The sadness Marcus felt for her the night of the party was the soul recognition of saying goodbye for good to the souls that were being left behind by being stagnant in their life and not evolving beyond their circumstances. The beauty was that Marcus's higher self elevated out enough just so his soul could come to Earth through Doris but not have to live as she had chosen for herself and her daughter. The threads of alcohol that were obviously in place with his biological mother didn't transfer over to him since Doris was never meant to be his real mom. She was merely the vehicle to get him here. Doris did right by Marcus when she gave him up, seeing that his life was beautiful, with a successful future ahead.

When we're experiencing something and wondering why it didn't work out the way we would've hoped, that's the ego talking. The higher self and our spirit guides have a plan for the best way to get us to our highest level of soul growth. In Marcus's case, he wondered why his birth mother didn't want him, then later realized he was grateful she didn't keep him. That heart filter was finally removed with the sweet realization that he was blessed.

A filter can be in the energy field for a variety of reasons. We place filters over various chakras to protect them. Some filters can be put in place by others. If there's a filter, it's important to continue the work to release it because if it's there too long, it can lead to health issues. I'm always glad when heart filters get released and dissolved, as I know they lead to heart attacks. A heart filter keeps us from self-love because when we put it in place, whether in a past life or this one, we deemed ourselves unlovable. When a soul continues to reincarnate, the filters that might have been applied during one life get carried to the next.

There was a woman named Leslie who came to me depressed about not being able to get pregnant. There was a visible filter over her sacral chakra that seemed to have been put in place several lifetimes ago. This happened to be within a two-week span of seeing several clients who were unable to conceive. I've come to accept that when the Universe wants me to learn something important, it's shown to me in various ways. So as Leslie began to tell her story and explain the sadness she had in not being able to be a mother, her spirit guides came in and said that it was because of an oath she had taken many lifetimes back. Her spirit guides showed how, in every lifetime since the oath, when given the opportunity to be in an adult female body, she could not conceive. So I knew we needed to see what happened when she made the oath, then remove it.

As I relaxed her by talking to her with her eyes closed, I asked if we could look at the lifetime that she carried the oath from and see what we needed to know. She regressed back to the life in what looked like London. It was around the year 1519. The scene opened with her in a small room, which felt like it might have been a basement. It felt unwelcoming—as if it were a secret location that many would be shocked about if it were found. She was sixteen years old and sewing what looked to be religious garments or robes. She seemed as clean as she could be considering the dwelling in which she was being kept.

"Leslie, do you know where we are?" I asked.

"We're in the room I live in."

As I stood in the room, it felt sad—as if she were never going to leave. Then her spirit guide stepped forward and said, "It was here she took the oath that she would never have another child." The scene changed quickly as a man in priest's robes came in. He was her uncle and was supposed to take care of her after her parents passed when she was five. After Leslie moved in with her uncle, she wasn't able to be out anywhere after she turned fourteen. He was a priest in hiding and worked to build the teachings of the Roman Catholic Church.

When I asked why she took the oath, it was shown she gave birth to fifteen children during her life, two of whom didn't make it and none of whom she was able to keep. Her uncle would take each one to the orphanage and say it had been left on the steps of the secret church. She hated him, and he kept her enslaved there until she died. Her oath not to have any more children was declared in that life as she was raped by her uncle and forced to mother children she didn't want.

As we were in that moment of witnessing what had happened, she was able to shift the filter, and it began to dissolve into the light of God. The sacral chakra was cleaned as it was boosted by healing light from her spirit guides. Just as I had been told, they couldn't do it until she released the oath she had made. After the session, the guides showed the spirit who was coming in to be born to her. With that message, I told her to expect the pregnancy in the next month or two.

If you're wondering if you have a filter somewhere in your energy field, I suggest grounding, allowing your guidance to verify, and then speaking aloud, asking your spirit guides and angels to remove the filter. You can use your hand to wipe away the energy around the area with the filter so it can move away. I've noticed that in sessions with clients, when I mention a filter, I've seen them swat it away. That begins to bring the emotions up and gives them the opportunity to finally start to clear.

Chapter 3

The Physical

Back in school, I remember a mom using the phrase, "You are who you run with." This was a subtle way of saying if you decide to be friends with those who are skipping school or using drugs, you will do the same. This is the truth, no matter your age or profession. You can absorb debris from another's energy field merely by walking past them in a restaurant, so imagine the impact the people you choose to spend the most time with will have on your field. Once you begin to become aware of the energies around you—or at least recognize an odd feeling you are having—

you can take the time you need to clear and recalibrate your energy field.

Think about a time when you may have met someone clingy or sleazy. Do you remember how you felt at the very moment your being first stood in front of their being? Even if you didn't shake their hand or touch them in any way, you felt their energy. How long did it take you to feel that you cleared the encounter?

EMS workers are people who provide emergency medical services at the scene of an accident or emergency of any kind. They must enter a scene from an emergency call, which is always a crapshoot. The scene could be something small or something very difficult to shake. The unshakable feeling is whatever became embedded in their field. The energies of these psychically and mentally strained situations also become embedded in the items used on these often-lifesaving missions. The materials such as blankets, chairs, and benches used inside emergency rescue vehicles, hospitals, and jails hold energy. The energy can be the nerves that were released by the people who were treated or held there.

Exercise #4

I would like you to make a list of places or people involved in experiences you've had that felt hard to shake. It doesn't matter how short of a moment it was—you need to disconnect these from your energy field. While making the list, you don't need to write a long explanation, just a reminder so the clearing can begin. To clear the effects of the experiences, we will focus on clearing the connection to the people and places on the list.

(Example: Ex-husband, Russell—was unfaithful in our marriage)

1)

_____

_____

2)

_____

_____

3)

_____

_____

4)

_____

_____

5)

_____

_____

6)

_____

_____

Sometimes when you acknowledge events and energy not belonging to you, a shift will begin, and the energy will return or be transmuted by the light and rendered uninhabited. This is ideally the way it should feel for any being who happens across a place that was once deemed traumatic. Once the place or space is cleared, it leaves the canvas open for a new interpretation and a clean slate to emit positive memories and actions.

When you think of a place that made you feel happy, you need to ask yourself: was the emotion coming from the experiences you had while you were there, or was it the energy that you felt there? When you begin to separate which feelings come from your personal experiences and preconceptions and which come from the true unfiltered energy of the actual place, you will start to understand the unspoken language of energy that many have no awareness of. The human view of energy is often mixed in with what the human eye has been taught. For example, many think that if someone lives in a beautiful mansion, their life must be happy. This isn't always the case, and it's one of the hardest things I've had to teach to another. It's also the thing that the frequency of God continues to point out that I'm to address in sessions with my clients. Once you begin to feel the energy without ego and human perception of what you think it is, then the truth comes in very smoothly. When you can do this continually, then and only then are you operating from the heart center. You need to know this is much harder when you're dealing with someone you're related to, and it's nearly impossible to do about someone you're in love with.

When humanity has imprinted trauma upon the Earth by committing a horrendous act of cruelty against a being, whether man or beast, it's embedded in that location until it's cleared. When this happens in any type of building, it takes more than just demolishing the building to remove the act created there. It takes a conscious effort in calling on Archangels, spirit guides, and Mother Earth for the clearing to begin. Once the energy is transmuted by the light, the event can still be viewed, but the emotions and horror will not be felt. When a building is demolished and hauled off to the dump, the energy in the material things is merely relocated, and the land still holds the very physical memory of the events that happened there.

Some years back in the hill country of Texas, a developer was surveying land to build on. The homes he had in mind were going to be in the price range of two to three million dollars. It was a picturesque terrain. While he was out looking it over, he called and asked me about the property he was thinking of buying. When I looked at the area, a few men of Spanish descent stood before me. They looked as though they'd been traveling and were seasoned adventurers. They showed me how they had camped in the area where the land developer was standing. The land was uninhabited at the time, and the vegetation was untouched. One had gathered some berries to eat with the dinner they shared. The berries were very toxic, and they never woke up. The small area of their campground still held their ambitions for adventure and for land to claim and their hopes to begin families. That land also held their sadness since they didn't know they were to go into the light. No one had come across them or stopped in the camp area long enough to see them before. I saw them standing, unscathed in their appearance despite the fact that their physical bodies were dust by then.

I asked what year it was. The one who went by the name Siglos answered, "1798." I was intrigued since the Spanish word *siglos* means "ages," yet none of them had aged at all. They were young and healthy in appearance—outside of the fact they were dead.

I called in the Archangels to open the portal so they could continue their spiritual journey and find the home they'd been searching for. I knew once they entered the portal, their true spiritual origin would be restored, and the experience of dying in the hill country of Texas would be a buried memory for them—but not for me. As the interaction was happening, I was describing most of it to the developer on the phone, yet he couldn't understand anything I was explaining.

After the call, I visited Siglos and his travel companions to see them restored in the light of God. I was shown the importance of clearing the sadness of them lingering for so long. It would help those who would eventually live on the property. If it had not been cleared, then anyone who lived in a house built on the ground of their campsite may not understand that the depression they were feeling wasn't their own and that it belonged to the lost travelers who had been stuck for so long.

My garage door opener broke, and the garage door was nearly impossible for me to open on my own. As I asked Siri for a garage door repairman in my area, one of the names stood out to me. I thought to myself, *Interesting—what could this be connected to?*

The repairman arrived. He was five foot eleven, lean, clean, and dressed as if he would be in an ad for a repairman but not actually look anything like the guy who would show up. The tag on his shirt read "Nathan." The overall color of his energy field origin was violet with interesting markings. As he stood on the doorstep, I also noticed a discoloration in his energy field from the bottom of his body up to his liver. That discoloration wasn't normal and indicated disease.

There was some dark shading in the liver region and spots on the root chakra. The dark shading was nearly black but not quite there. The black spots in the field indicated cancer.

I opened the side door for him, and he explained the repair and new door opener as he set up his ladder in the center of the garage. I sat on the stoop of the side door to the garage, where I was looking up as he did the installation. He began making conversation and asked what I did. The frequency of God came in and said to watch his field while he talked. I explained that I read the body and saw conception to death. He seemed to want to shake off what I said by avoiding eye contact. Then he began to explain what was going on in his life. He said he'd been having issues with his small intestine. As he was telling me this, I got a flash of him in another country with other soldiers. He was surveying land for an outpost or what some may know as a miniature military base. The land chosen wasn't soil-tested, and the dirt was highly toxic. The area was dusty, and even the best-built building or tent couldn't keep the people from breathing the toxic dust into their bodies.

I sat there in surprise over the footage of his life I was viewing, and I heard him say, "Are you okay?" I moved my eyes from his feet to his face and asked him how long he'd been in the military. With a surprised look, he asked, "How did you know I was in the military? Most people are surprised when I tell them I served." I think the conversation was distracting because he realized he'd missed a step and had to take off the part he had worked hard to get into place. "What are you, a witch too?" he said as if he were trying to hide the fear that was creeping up.

The frequency of God came in, and this time, it urged me to encourage him not to wait and to go through the process to clear the issues with a series of specialists. So I blurted out, "I know you're putting off seeking a diagnosis for what you're experiencing, but it's important you get on this now and get to a couple of specialists. The faster this is addressed, the faster the shift in the energy can begin and you can get this behind you."

"Really?" he said. "That can't be the way it works since there are people who do everything and still die."

Trying to calm him with the energy of my words, I explained, "Everyone is different; everyone has different things that they are working to shift in their own energy field and life. There's one right way for each person, and yours is connected to releasing guilt over the location you chose as an outpost for those soldiers." The wrench fell from his hands, hitting the floor, then landing next to me. He stared at me for a moment while reaching into his tool belt for another.

The installation was done, and as he folded the ladder, I felt he was still replaying my words in his head, as he seemed miles away from me. He synced the garage door main box to the garage door remote and handed it to me. The garage door opened, and he walked to his truck to get the receipt book from his dash. He got inside with his truck door open and began to write out the receipt. Then, while staring at the paper and pen, he said his wife had been on him to get to a doctor, and he'd been making excuses not to schedule appointments to avoid going. He halfway laughed and said, "What if insurance doesn't pay it all, and I have to dip into my son's college fund?"

"What? Now I know you're just digging for an excuse not to go." I tried to make him laugh and, while smiling, said, "Your son won't be attending college. He'll choose a different direction." I knew he needed something solid to go on to take the leap to his healing path ahead, so I explained that when I saw someone who was going to pass, if I knew they didn't want to get better and they were determined to accept their out, then my only words would be to get their affairs in order. I added, "My words to you, Nathan, are to release the guilt you carry and change the dynamics of what was done. You can do this by merely releasing what you don't want and replacing it with what you do want. Your wife wants to go to Hawaii, so make it your vision that you'll take care of this issue and take her there. Here's a list of suggestions to follow along with your doctor's advice."

A few weeks went by, and upon coming home one evening, there was a flier on the door from Nathan's Garage Door Service. There was a large arrow across the ad illustrating to turn over the page, where there was a written message that read:

I stopped by to let you know I am feeling great and have seen a few doctors that said I came in just in time. I am using my child's college fund to take wifey to Hawaii and give her the vacation of her dreams. We are both grateful for your guidance.

Aloha, Nathan

The energy of guilt over the location he had chosen for a base needed to be shifted to an understanding that, since he had no idea about the toxicity of the land, it wasn't something to allow the feelings of guilt to fester over. The origin of the guilt could easily be released once he was ready.

The stories above all had energy attachments to places and events. These types of attachments need to be cleared too. They can be something small, such as a visit, or they can be something big, such as guilt over a decision you made for others at a specific location.

In eighth grade, my best friend had a major crush on a guy named Kurt, and while he knew he was handsome, he never showed any interest in dating. He walked with a heavy energy discoloration over his back and across his heart. The energy causing the discoloration was due to an event that had happened in this life.

In social studies one day, the teacher separated us into a four-person group where we were to conduct a study. At the time, my right wrist was broken. It wasn't just broken—it had been cast old-school style, heavy in plaster and resting in a sling. I must have looked helpless because he was willing to lift my books, get my paper out, and open my notebook. As he helped me, it was the first time since I had known him that his energy shifted. It was as if his act of helping me at that moment was earning him some sort of reward. I knew he wasn't interested in me nor I in him, but he was genuinely happy to help.

The assignment was to compare the home dynamics of one- or two-parent households to extended-family households. As we began to draw a chart to compare the characteristic roles of family members and the dwellings in which they lived, like a house or apartment, I noticed Kurt's energy change. His field became murky.

As soon as I noticed, I volunteered to go first and said, "I live with both of my parents and two siblings." Deja, sitting next to me, said she lived with her grandmother since both of her parents were in prison. Brian said he had six siblings and lived with both of his parents, an aunt, and a grandparent.

Then it was Kurt's turn. I saw the murky color move to his head region, almost encompassing the entirety of his body while in the sitting position. He began by saying he lived with his younger sister, Maura, who he called monkey, and his mom. He was the caregiver for his sister while his mother worked. His eyes began to tear up, and I noticed all of us had leaned in as if we were about to hear a secret. He began to speak slowly—like he was going to say something no one else in the world had ever heard. He explained that one night while watching his little sister, he had put a pot of water on the stove to boil to make her mac and cheese. He told her, "When the water begins to boil, I'll add the noodles." The phone rang, and it was a girl he liked talking to. He had forgotten about the water and his little sister. He heard the pot hit the floor in the kitchen, followed by bloodcurdling screams. He rushed in to find that his sister had pulled the pot down to check if it was time to add the noodles. Half of her face was covered in third-degree burns, and she would have to endure skin grafts to restore her skin. His eyes were red as he said her face was forever scarred because he didn't watch her properly.

The energy in his field shifted, and at the time, though I didn't understand how, I felt there was a healing that had occurred in his talking about it. I knew him for several years after, and no one from that group ever talked about it with him again. We all were part of his energy shift in helping him heal from some of the guilt of that night. It made so much sense why he didn't attend after-school activities or entertain girls who were trying to get his attention. After I began working with others in cases like Kurt's, I was reminded of his story, and when I asked how he was healing, God said, "He refuses to release the guilt completely, though sharing his story has helped him do better than he would have otherwise."

In Kurt's case, he had threads to the event even though he wasn't personally injured. Therefore, when you're working through events in your own life to clear the connection, don't ignore things you may be tempted to brush off because they didn't physically happen to you. It may be something you witnessed or are still connected to on an emotional level of some sort.

Chapter 4

The Dancers

When we visit a place or partake in events, the effects may linger in our energy field.

The etheric reminders may not be seen by the eye but are perhaps felt. These cords, markings, and tethers are in the energy field until we elevate our energy to a higher vibration by emotional exercises that raise our frequency. Raising our frequency can be done by frequently engaging in release activities, such as cord cleaning and grounding to the Earth. When we ground to the Earth, it doesn't remove what we aren't ready to release until the moment we open to the possibility that the lower frequency lives we've been living no longer match the higher vibrations our energy fields now carry.

When I share an experience, it's the best way to teach since it allows those who may not recall something important to have the memory triggered by the story. Some people may have an epiphany with a teaching moment I share. You know by now that I like to explain *how* I know something rather than saying, "This is the answer."

When I began working with clients, I would tell them the things I was seeing. Some would leave with the feeling that what I'd said made no sense at the time of the session, only to find out that it all became clear when something related happened later. They would come back and say, "How did you know?" So now, without having to explain each time I'm with a client, I hope they'll take the information I give them with the understanding that there's an experience I went through to know what I'm teaching.

Years back when I worked for a restaurant, I was shown many things that I didn't understand at that time. Those experiences would later be referenced by my own spirit guides in psychic readings while I was with clients.

When I'd only been working there for three days, I didn't know the regulars, so they would be pointed out by the other waitresses and bartenders. The place was very nice, with a full dinner menu, low lighting, and a small dance floor. Our uniforms were tuxedo shirts, black shorts, bow ties, and cummerbunds. It would be better described as an off-brand Morton's Steakhouse with a nightclub feel. The place had a protective energy about it that I came to understand later.

The hostess at the door had the sections of the restaurant on a rotation, so when we came in, there was a chart, and each section was assigned a waitress. This meant when a customer walked in, the hostess would seat them in the first section, then the next customer would be seated in the next section, and so forth until the tables were full. This was the standard rule unless a customer requested a certain waitress.

It was a great place to work. There was very little turnover in the staff—one of the waitresses had been there sixteen years. Her name was Samantha, and she was the lead waitress. Her energy was tired, and she carried a dark, murky green over her back. Samantha made the schedules for everyone, along with the floor section chart. She was very nice and only worked day shifts. She didn't favor anyone—begging wouldn't get us the preferred section of the restaurant. We were never guaranteed the same one.

One day, I waited eagerly in the waitress well, which was a term used to describe the place waitresses stood and refilled drinks next to the bar or in a cubby near a register. I stacked the napkins just right on my tray and put a few pens in my pocket to jot large orders down. Two waitresses named Stacy and Renee were standing behind me. They both had very cloudy and gray energy in various patches. I overheard Stacy say, "Oh great, look what just walked in and is headed to my station."

I glanced up and noticed a group of women dressed very nicely and laughing as they were being guided to a table. Thinking about the comment from Stacy, I turned around and said, "What's wrong with them?" I knew their words stemmed from jealousy but wanted to hear what their answer would be.

They both leaned in and together explained that the group of women were dancers who worked at the topless bar up the road.

"Are you kidding?" I commented, glaring at them while understanding that prejudice had many different facets.

Stacy smiled and said, "If you want them, you can wait on them, and I'll take your next table that gets seated."

"Of course, I'll take them," I said as I thought, *I came in today to work.* I couldn't see why she wouldn't want to wait on them. I walked up to the table and introduced myself, then took their order. They ordered dinner and drinks and said a few guys would be joining them. My station was packed in no time since the dinner crowd had hit. I didn't let any tables suffer as I stayed on their refills and kept the tables clean.

When I dropped the check by, the women asked for my name again and said they would request me when they came back. When they got ready to leave, I was standing by the door talking to Evan, the owner of the restaurant. I turned around and thanked them for coming in. One of the girls hugged Evan and told him out of all the times they had come for dinner, that was the best service they'd ever received. When they left, I went to the table to clean and move everything back into place. When I went to the waitress station to put the tab and money in the register, there was a note on the tab that read, *You are very nice and an incredible waitress. The extra money is all yours—we will see you soon. Shelby.* Their tab was $432, and they'd left me $1,000. I recounted the money and reread the note—they had left me a $568 tip. While I was still in the afterglow of this generous gesture, Stacy walked up to the station. I thought perhaps I should thank her for letting me wait on the ladies who had originally been seated in her station. Before I could, Stacy leaned over and told me, "Thank you for taking my table."

As I was in shock, I answered, "Are you serious? What do you have against them?"

Stacy, with her murky red-gray energy field, laughed and said, "Nothing, I just don't want to wait on people who do that for a living. If you don't mind, you can wait on them anytime they get seated in my station."

A week went by, and the ladies came back; this time, the hostess sat them in my station. As I approached the table, they were so happy to see me. I had a packed station, and every table was a delight to wait on. The funny thing about it was that every table was sat with regular guests who the other wait staff seemed to make comments about. I had to wonder what the heck they were doing working in a restaurant if they were so critical of those they waited on. I came to work to do my job, and I loved the people I waited on. Every table was ordering dinner and drinks. Shelby and the ladies had requested a table for six right next to a guy named Steve, who requested the server to cut up his steak. I noticed he didn't ogle them, and when the hostess walked him to his seat, his energy was focused more on his happiness with the table he was seated at because it overlooked the dance floor.

As I was in the waitress well ordering drinks for those in my station, Stacy nudged me and, laughing, said in a teasing voice, "The creepy Steve and the girls from the club are all in your station. Have fun." She walked away to check her tables while my eyes stayed focused on the bartender making the drinks, and her crazy laugh began to fade. I delivered all the drinks and realized the food for a few tables was ready. One belonged to Steve, so I cut up his food as I would do for myself and walked it out. I delivered it with a smile and asked if he needed anything else. He looked at his plate, and instantly I saw that he was happy—the golden energy in his field brightened. He sat up taller and said, "No, thank you, this looks great."

When the night was over and I was cleaning my station, I found Shelby's bracelet under the table. It was a diamond tennis bracelet. I knew it was valuable and thought it should be locked in the cash register or safe. I showed it to the bartender, Dante, and asked if he could lock it in the safe when he counted his drawer. He knew how some of the other female employees felt about Shelby's lifestyle and suggested that I drop it by her club the next evening on my way to work. Dante was a hard worker and carried a beautiful green light in his energy. The green hue in his field meant he was honest, trustworthy, and had the ability to teach since the people who carried this hue of green were often patient when it came to teaching. I knew he struggled with alcoholism, but he was fair and had a conscience. In the short time I'd been working, I witnessed some of the waitresses doing shady stuff, and I could tell he didn't approve.

The next evening on my way to work, I stopped by Shelby's club to leave the bracelet for her. When I got out of my car, I could see the doorman, who happened to carry a long mark in his energy field across his throat. When I got to the door, I asked if Shelby had already arrived. He asked what I wanted from Shelby, and as I began to explain, she and two of the other girls, Marissa and Tamika, came to the door and told him I was their waitress and to let me in. They were very welcoming and offered me a drink. I told them I found the bracelet when I was cleaning up the night before and didn't want to leave it with the restaurant. Shelby was thrilled to have it back and had been upset that she'd lost it. I could see the happiness in her heart as she held the bracelet to her before motioning to one of the girls for help to get it back on.

Tamika asked what time I was going to work. Her energy was different from the other women there—she had geometric symbols in her field, which led me to understand she had a scientific origin to her. Marissa said, "Well, you have some time, and they just put out the buffet, so why don't you get a plate, and I'll get you a 7UP." I agreed, as I was hungry and hadn't eaten yet. You see, the great thing about working at a restaurant was that we got a meal for our shift. The problem was on Friday and Saturday, it was so packed, we never got a break. So I was happy they offered. I got a plate and sat down. No one was there except a couple of guys far on the other side. The girls all gathered around to talk while I ate. I noticed a guy motioning for Marissa to come over. I knew Tamika presented a helpless sense about her—perhaps it was to attract guys—but after seeing those shapes in her field, I knew she was NASA-level smart. She could out-calculate anyone. As Marissa wandered away, I glanced up while in conversation with Tamika to see Marissa's energy field. She had several thousand threads coming from various parts of her body. I had seen threads like that before but not as many as Marissa's. Most adults had them. I even had a few in various spots.

After about thirty minutes, Marissa emerged from the back of the stage. Her energy was scattered. The energy field itself was very distracting to me because I'd never seen someone in that circumstance. Of course, I knew she must have just had sex with the guy who had called her over, even though she didn't want to. I realized I had the opportunity to see the difference between someone who wanted to engage with love and desire and those who did it for money. I sat there, wishing I could ask her to turn for me so I could see any other new markings in her energy field that maybe I missed. There may have been other colorations or markings from her recent activities in the back room. I heard the frequency say, "This is what it looks like when you allow someone to use your body and there's no heart connection."

I glanced up at Shelby as she thanked me again for returning her bracelet. Her field had a beautiful pink that ran around the heart and around her hands. When I got ready to leave, they all walked me to the door and had the doorman walk me to my car. On the way to work, I thought about Marissa's energy. *So the threads in various spots must be from sex.* The frequency said, "Not all are, and you will see the difference."

Over the next few weeks working at the restaurant, I came to love my customers, and I think they loved me too. They would request to sit in my station, and when no tables were available, they would wait at the bar until one opened. There were a few times when people at an existing table would offer their empty seats up for other customers to join. I loved nights when everything harmonized together and customers were treating each other like family. I realized I was offering to work at wedding receptions and other private parties because it gave me a sense of belonging that I hadn't felt before.

The owner, Evan, would get handsy with a few girls who worked there, but he didn't with me. I felt he respected me because I was there every day and was never late or slaked off. Evan was Chinese and taught me about many of his traditions, including always calling me into the kitchen to teach me how to make special dishes.

One Saturday when I was working, I was very hungry. I understood that when the place was packed, we may have to pass on a real break, which was normally the time I used for eating. I was feeling weak, and as soon as I thought about sitting down, I woke up in Evan's office. I was lying on the floor, and before I could fully understand what had happened, a waitress and Evan were standing over me, and Evan was holding my hand. A guy from the kitchen walked in with a plate of food, and Evan began to feed it to me while the waitress propped me up. His energy was of concern, but at that moment, I heard the frequency of the creator say, "Look at his heart." As I began eating what he was feeding me, I noticed a warm pink energy cord come from his heart chakra to me, and it began to blend. The frequency came in and said, "This is what family love looks and feels like—when a loving, caring cord connects." I sat up with the new things that I had just learned in mind and had a deeper love for Evan and that place.

When I was finished eating the meal Evan had fed me, I returned to the dining area to get back to work. Jeff, one of the bartenders, asked if I was okay to work, and I explained that I was feeling so much better now that I had eaten.

Evan walked up to me, and in a very firm voice, he said, "Don't go so long without eating; I don't want my waitresses falling over. Now get back to work."

Jeff motioned for me to lean in and said when I fell over, the people who'd jumped up to check on me were all pushed aside when Evan heard it was me, and he alone picked me up and carried me back to his office. I knew he had a tough exterior, but since I saw that pink cord from his heart, I knew he loved me in his Evan way.

I began to put together other times I noticed cords. There were good cords that formed out of a place of love, including family cords. Then there were cords that attached when a person allowed someone to use them in various ways, like abuse cords. Those cords would attach where the person's body experienced the interaction most acutely. I thought back to childhood and times when I'd experienced abuse. There was always something extra that began to form in my field or on the part of my body that endured the pain. It was the same for emotional abuse—the cords would appear in various places.

Later that week, while I was working, Shelby came in and requested a large table for eight. After I moved tables together, she sat down, and I went to get her drink. When I returned, I asked if Marissa and Tamika would be joining her. She told me Tamika would be there and named a few people I hadn't really met before. I recognized the name Heather. "Heather is the one who dressed like a gypsy when you came in with a group, right?"

She laughed. "The story behind that getup is that she was a waitress before she became a full-time dancer, and when she would clean up after closing, she would find wedding bands just about every night under the tables and chairs. She began a 'lost men's wedding rings' collection."

"That's crazy. I didn't realize so many guys lost their wedding rings there."

Shelby laughed a short giggle. "Yes, they lose them when they slip them off to appear single, and sometimes the rings miss their pockets and drop to the floor."

At that moment, a group walked up to the table. The group was a mix of dancers and three guys who looked like they had just walked out of a medical convention. One of the guys had a very distinguished appearance. There was an alarming discoloration that ran from the top of his head down the left side of his face. I heard the frequency say, "This is a drug addiction that you're seeing, and the left side indicates the nostril he uses most often for cocaine." I knew no one else could see this. He sat down next to Shelby and ordered a drink. He appeared to be hypnotized by her and seemed to hang on her every word. I brought drinks out to the table and looked at the other guys. They all had medical symbols in their energy fields, which indicated they were doctors. The other two didn't have cocaine markings in their energy fields, nor did they seem acquainted with the party lifestyle.

When Shelby's date got up to go to the bathroom, she leaned over to tell me he was the guy who gave her the diamond bracelet and then explained that he was a heart doctor. That confirmed my first read on the group about the medical symbols. My human perception would not have thought I would encounter a heart doctor with a cocaine addiction. There was a cord that attached around the top of his head and flowed off to the left. That was the cord to the addiction and supplier.

When I was serving, Shelby told Heather to show me the belt. Heather shook her head and laughed, embarrassed and yet proud to show me. She reached down into her purse under the table. I noticed some cords attached to the back of her head and the middle of her back. She pulled up a half-inch belt that she had slipped the wedding rings onto; the end had a cork from a wine bottle with a slit in the middle, and that, too, was on the belt. The belt was buckled so no rings slipped off.

I was amazed at how many there were. "How many rings do you have?" I asked with wide eyes.

Heather's laugh reminded me of Marilyn Monroe in *Some Like It Hot*. As she smiled big, jiggling the belt in a boastful way, she said, "Almost ninety rings; there's room for more, and we all know I'll find some." Then she laughed and put it back in her bag. The belt itself had Heather attached to the ring collection by a cord the same way I'd seen with a child to a security blanket.

As I reached to clean up the table, I asked Heather, "How long have you been collecting rings?"

She said, "Eighteen months. The first six months, I waited tables and found them when cleaning."

After dinner, Shelby's date gestured for the tab. I walked it up, and he said, "Just a minute," pulling out what looked to be five thousand dollars. He carefully counted five one-hundred-dollar bills out, then Shelby looked at him and said, "You need to give her at least a four-hundred-dollar tip. She's our waitress." As he looked down at his hand, I saw that there was a dark line that ran down the back of his head, which indicated an addiction that separated him from his life path or the mission of his soul. I could also see that he would never break the addiction. The darker line along the discoloration from the addiction indicated he would die soon of something else since he was too far off his spiritual mission to complete what he came here for.

Because of what I had seen when I visited the club where Shelby and the girls worked and saw Marissa go to the private room with a customer. I'd learned that paid sex activities affected the energy field. When people entered the room, their energy field was much different than the way it looked after, depending on what occurred and for what reason. It not only changed based on what they engaged in, but it also absorbed some of the energy of the room itself.

In the world of topless clubs, there's usually at least one room where dancers can take a client. The rooms have a mixture of heavy energies that would be nearly impossible to clear with techniques used in clearing spaces. This is due to the cords that the visitors to the room may still have tethered to them. This is a very small example of the threads to behavior or emotions that spaces and land may hold. When we partake in actions that may not be for the good of our beings or others', those tethers are there until we remove them or until we raise our frequency to see past actions differently.

The markings in the energy fields of the dancers I knew included threads and cords from people they had only one experience with several years back. I also learned that, even when they would say it was a one-time thing that occurred between them and another person, any time one of them needed an energy lift from either being sick or depressed, they could feed off the energy cords that became connected after that one-time interaction. This is the reason why many in industries that interact on a physical level feel drained and more weighed down by others' energy than those who work alone or in a setting with one or two other people. The fields of physical therapy and chiropractic medicine are two examples of very physical jobs that tend to invite corded energy from others. These are just a few occupations that should make clearing a daily or weekly thing.

Exercise #5

Now that you've read this story, I would like you to think about anyone else who you might add to the list of those you've formed cords with. Also think about buildings or land that you may have cords to. If you can't sense the cord, I would like you to refer to the name of the person or building in the list you made in Chapter 3. Remember that cords form with just about everyone you are related to and those you have had connections to in the world outside of your family. Some of the those cords can be healthy attachments that form when we care about each other, like the pink love cord I felt from Evan after I fainted. Other cords harbor pain. For the purpose of this exercise, we will only be focusing on the cords that carry harmful energy. The cords to spaces, homes, buildings, ideas, beliefs, and land form where experiences have been tethered to trauma, sadness, and guilt (see Figure 3). The cord clearing will need to be done on every person and space that you feel is a negative interaction or memory you want to clear. The memory of something being good and bad is a human perception we store in those cords. The cleaning will allow acceptance, and you will come to see the experience as a step toward your goal of balanced spiritual perception. The ability to clean the cord once and for all is indicated when you see you're ready to release emotion from that interaction and move forward. Then and only then does the cord stay clean. After you're honestly able to say the emotions are clear, then the cord can be removed forever. Until then, no one and nothing can remove the cord.

*Refer back to Chapter 1—Cord cleaning 101 when you're ready to start clearing these people, places, and things.

Figure 3—Cords attached: people, places, words spoken to you, and things you witnessed.

Chapter 5

The Marriage

The marriage agreement is only an earthly experience at the time of writing this book. On most other planets, the beings who live in harmony know when they've found their match, as it is easily identifiable to them. It's not the same as Earth, where there's so much pressure and so much doubt. Here, there are those who marry to change their position in life, and that, of course, doesn't exist on the higher-level planets since all beings harmonize at the love frequency, and there is no cheating or divorce. The beings living there know each other instantly as they see the energy field, and while humans can lie with their mouths, their energy fields will always tell the truth. There have been other planets in the past that had relationship struggles like humanity, but those planets are no longer in existence and no longer host lifeforms to hold souls so they can have experiences like on Earth. Those on the higher-level planets see their partner as their equal and their teammate and would not have a desire to seek a moment of self-indulgence with another to ruin the bond. This is one way those in the human system fail each other. The other is through teaching false ideas about marriage within church walls. There are some who believe that when you are sealed by a union, you are forever bonded together on the other side, and that isn't true. The people you marry are often soul members of your soul group, and those are going to play out in other lifetimes as other people you may know.

Those from the fundamentalist Mormon religion believe that if a man has multiple wives, he is sealed with them for eternity. This is not true; it's a man-made belief to make one gender be seen as the stronger one. The fundamentalist Mormons are not the only ones who have taught this—I'm merely using them as an example. The teaching that males are the leaders in faith and family has been used to keep females down. It was designed to keep the hierarchy arranged so those who possess physical strength have the power as the leaders.

The original view of women was amazement at their ability to physically bring other beings into the world through reproduction.

Women were seen as great beings until men decided too much power had been shown to the female aspect of humanity and that they didn't want females to dominate. Many women were enslaved by their families who were frightened by the early churches, and governing councils began to double down on their teachings. The story of Adam and Eve was told in a way to make Eve the villain. This put guilt into all females that perhaps we screwed things up for all of humanity. The teachings began to be the word of man. It was thought that if Eve made a bad choice, then it wasn't a good idea for females to make other choices. And since the females produce children, they should just mind the children and care for the men.

It was also the strength in the physical that led to the domineering teachings of one being greater than another. Therefore, when soldiers would go into villages to kill, they would rape the women. Similarly, when dogs show domination, they hump your leg. They are not seeking a physical release as a human would with masturbation, they are seeking a mental one.

Where did this come from? It came from those who visited and took humanity out of the utopia that the creator had for us, which many refer to as Eden. The soldiers or groups of people who attack others by means of rape are carrying the heavy threads of the split from God. These threads release when they forgo the desire to rape or attack another with their procreational parts. When a situation comes up, it is often a repeat to see if you will do the same in the next life, and it's meant for you always to take the high road and not give in to the lower frequencies.

I'm not sure at what point my mom knew or worried that I could tell she wasn't being honest—perhaps it was when she realized I just knew things. At that point, she doubled down about how great her mom was. I suppose from a human perspective, Mom's mom, who I refer to as my Mamaw, was a wonderful person who was a victim of arranged marriage. She was depressed her whole life and tried to make the best of the situation. Mamaw had a filter over her heart in her energy field that was put there in this lifetime because of the arranged marriage.

People place fear and judgment on each other because of the pressure of culture and the teachings of the church. This was set up in a way that stole a person's value, as they could be traded without consent. The concept behind arranged marriage is that a female is not of value without a man to own her. The belief is a key among some churches that see it as an opportunity for families to grow and expand their congregation and keep the religion alive for generations. There are many cultures that still practice arranged marriages, and they feel it's the only way to have a blessing from the couple's parents. Depending on the religious teachings of the faith you were born into, you may have been provided a very shady benchmark to something that should have been beautiful and felt out by only the two people whose souls want to marry and not the community, church, or family. There have been many religious affiliations that not only set rules for who can marry and how, but they even decided that the male gender should be the head or govern the home. This is still a common belief—even in institutions that do not publicly proclaim it.

Before the sixties, marriage was glamorized as the next step in a young woman's life. In many cultures, it's frowned upon to have a daughter who's unmarried. This was a stronghold method used to work on the psyche of females all over the world. It's still embedded in many of our sisters who believe they are nothing without a man to love them.

The young men don't have it easy, as it was determined they were to marry and be the head of their family. What does that even mean? When you're balancing your spiritual walk, you will realize that it becomes easy to drop the old identifying gender roles that have been impressed upon us. When anyone is pushed into a marriage for the wrong reasons, it will never feel good to either person.

Exercise #6-a

Now I want you to think about the first time you heard about or were given an explanation of marriage. Think about keywords and the people who spoke about them. Consider your understanding of those individuals and the explanation they gave you. I also want you to think about the union they may have been in at that time.

Your first views of marriage (Example: Forever, something expected of you, faithful, joy):

_____

_____

_____

_____

_____

_____

_____

_____

The person or people who explained marriage and their unions at the time (Example: Parents, TV):

_____

_____

_____

_____

_____

_____

_____

_____

Your adult view of marriage (Example: Progress, happiness, next step, evolution, expected):

_____

_____

_____

_____

_____

_____

_____

_____

Marriages that you've had (Example: Sally during college):

_____

_____

_____

_____

_____

_____

_____

_____

The truth of marriage as you see it (Example: Complicated, requires work, can be joyful):

_____

_____

_____

_____

_____

_____

_____

_____

Good examples of marriage that you've witnessed firsthand (Example: Grandparents):

_____

_____

_____

_____

_____

_____

_____

_____

Bad examples of marriage that you've witnessed firsthand (Example: Sister, myself):

_____

_____

_____

_____

_____

_____

_____

_____

When we are fresh and new to the world that we know as Earth, our memories are wiped clean of any past life experiences. While our memory may be wiped clean, our soul carries markings and trauma from other lifetimes. These experiences, if they were traumatic, can affect the relationships you experience in this life. We often have no idea why we may sabotage a great connection or be drawn in by narcissistic mates. There are various reasons why our higher self brings certain encounters across our paths. Some of these reasons may be to see our self-worth, recognize what we don't want, or complete a situation we were never able to choose before when we last saw the soul we are crossing paths with again in this life.

Exercise #6-b

Take this space and write the names of people who came to mind when reading the last passage. Let's focus on all those relationships that you have experienced yourself and those that you have witnessed. Were they good ones who you let go on by, or were they ones who helped you to recognize you are worth more? It's not important to spend time reminiscing now; just make the list, and let's move forward.

Good relationships (Example: My friend Jody, Uncle Bob):

_____

_____

_____

_____

_____

_____

_____

_____

Not-so-great relationships that I learned from (Example: Parents, past marriage):

_____

_____

_____

_____

_____

_____

_____

_____

When you glance back at the first explanation of marriage and consider who gave you the explanation, you may sit and laugh at what they told you. You might look at the explanation and see that it came through the eyes of a jaded person. The examples of good and bad marriages you listed would have been your foundation for the idea of marriage. As you continue to get older, your views and concepts change because of what you experience. Each one of these examples, good or bad, is etched in your energy field. You may be wondering how a marriage you only witnessed but weren't a part of can end up in your energy field. The energy field is very large. It's much bigger than your body, and if you were sitting in another room and the couple had an emotionally charged interaction, then their energy still affected your field. The notes and memories you recalled about marriage may be things you hadn't thought of in a while, or perhaps they reflect a vision you hold close and think of often. Writing down the beliefs and assumptions you've been taught allows you to sort through what is truth and what is an illusion based on others' perceptions.

What I learned of marriage as a child

When I was five years old, I overheard Mom and Dad talking about my favorite uncle. Let me give you some backstory about Uncle Dave. He was almost two years younger than Dad, and while Dad was serving in the Air Force, Uncle Dave joined the Army. After Uncle Dave's tour in Vietnam, he received a permanent change of station (PCS). He was twenty years old when he arrived at his new post in Germany, and while he lived there, he met a native German named Marilee. She had one daughter from a previous relationship named Christine. It wasn't long before Marilee and Uncle Dave married. When he didn't reenlist, they all moved to Texas. Uncle Dave knew Christine needed a father figure, and since he'd lost his father—my grandfather—when he was only fifteen, he wanted to give Christine a great life. Marilee had other plans. Her energy field was bright red with orange highlighting on the outer edge. I understood this to mean that she was root chakra driven, which later, as an adult, I came to understand meant sex was the driving force behind her focus to obtain what she wanted. We all later learned she continued to communicate with a man in German and eventually went back to Germany, and she and Uncle Dave filed for divorce.

When I was very young, I was not often around my Uncle Dave since he was still in the Army, and his visits were rare. I remember meeting Christine and seeing a love for her and her mother in my uncle's energy field. Christine saw herself as an accessory, and when I saw her energy field, I could tell she lacked the unconditional love from her mother that I lacked from mine. Uncle Dave had a heart connection to them both and was true to that connection. He had a beautiful green energy field with a stream of pink light that flowed through the field from up above. I wasn't sure where it came from at the time, but I noticed being around him felt good. I remember seeing the pink love light emitting from his heart to everyone he met—I noticed it every time he was in communication with another person. He would tell me stories of times he and other soldiers taught the children in the villages in Vietnam how to play baseball.

After his divorce, he remained open to love but continued to make poor choices for partners. I knew he wanted a wife, and it didn't matter if she had kids—he would want them too. He wanted a relationship like the one he witnessed between his parents, which was complete devotion. When Grandfather Teddy worked, Grammy worked with him. My father and my uncle witnessed that type of love and dedication. I knew Uncle Dave was seeking that type of relationship. He didn't care to have children of his own since he worried about dying young and leaving them to suffer as he and my father did after their dad passed away.

He continued to fall in love fast and get married quickly. After the third time he went through love and then divorce and heartbreak, I recall a conversation my dad had with him. Dad said, "David, take your time and get to know someone; stop feeling you must get married." Whenever I saw Uncle Dave, I wondered if I'd be introduced to new cousins from a marriage he may be entering between our visits with him. When we would show up to visit, I never knew whether the same woman would be with him. As a kid, I wasn't given any updates unless we were en route to Uncle Dave's and would be meeting someone new.

After my father passed, Uncle Dave married again—and again, he felt he was in love. That time, the person he married was looking for anyone so she could have someone provide for her, and she seemed to have just as many marriages under her belt. Her energy was dark with a brown color—as if nothing anyone could say or do could soften her heart. She was as rough as unfinished wood and helped me later understand that some of the various markings in a field were from lessons unlearned in a repeating pattern. It was she that I came to use as a benchmark when measuring others who could never evolve beyond their current mindset in life. That meant that no matter who they met and what they did, the individual wouldn't discover what they needed to in this life experience, and it would take another life to get the lesson learned. I also understood that Uncle Dave, by his human perception, thought he could love her so much that she would change and see that love was real and just accept it. When her actions were colder than he could understand, he took a job driving rigs and was frequently on the road. It was that occupation that I believe allowed the marriage to last longer than any of his others. While he hadn't learned that his choice in women was based on his need to fix, he thought he was getting older, so there was no need to divorce. Shortly after he made that decision, he was diagnosed with prostate cancer. While he went to the doctor alone and wasn't able to go on long drives, his wife would laugh at him on days he couldn't move. She would cook and not feed him. He would get the energy up to find something to eat, and she would laugh.

Uncle Dave called me and told me he had my Grammy's jewelry box and a doll with some family pictures he wanted me to have. I asked how he was doing, and when I heard her yell in the background, I heard a frequency telling me Uncle Dave wasn't eating and had given up. I asked him if he had seen his doctor, and he explained it was a drive and he would go when he knew he could make it. His wife at the time told him she wouldn't drive him and that he would die anyway. I told him how much I missed him and that I felt he would be better here in Houston since the VA hospital was close and there were better doctors to help him on his journey. He soon packed his camper and headed my way.

When he got to my place, his energy field had changed greatly since the last time I had seen him face-to-face, which had been about six years. The beautiful green that shined bright had become worn in spots, and other colors had mixed in from various angles of his field. The pink was the only thing that was the same. He was so happy to see us, as I was him. I asked him to tell me stories about my Grammy that I didn't know. We found him a doctor's office nearby, which I drove him to every week. His energy didn't seem to shift much. I cooked healthy meals, trying to get the energy to change back to what I knew him to be, but nothing shifted.

One of his cousins, Chris, lived nearby and wanted my uncle to move in with him since he had plenty of room. I knew it was the right move since Chris had space and my uncle didn't want to die at my house with the kids there. The kids and I visited every other day, trying to be mindful and respectful of Chris. One Thursday morning, as we were talking, I noticed Dave's energy field was leaking light and that relatives and loved ones were beginning to gather. This gathering told me they had come to help him cross over. I realized he couldn't see them, perhaps from what he had been given by the hospice nurse for the pain. I could see them, but there was no communication with me—none. I knew who they were and why they were there, and since there was no explanation needed, there was only a message of a frequency acknowledgment that they had come for him. My father was there with his mother. They had the same look on their face as if they were waiting for a bus or a train, and there was no need for a personal visit with me. They were there for him. I touched his hand and could still see the pink that streamed from him to me, and I knew that would be goodbye. Later that night,

Chris called me and told me that Uncle Dave had passed. I heard frequency confirm that Uncle Dave has crossed and was home.

On the day of Uncle Dave's funeral, Chris came over to inform me that he'd reached out to Uncle Dave's wife and told her he had passed, and she'd replied, "Okay, please send a copy of the death certificate for the insurance policy," and then hung up. I remembered what I'd first seen in her energy field when I was younger and didn't know much about the energy field. I wished I could talk to Uncle Dave.

When I arrived home, I heard the frequency say, "Allow your uncle's spirit to rebuild from the destruction that happened during his life on Earth." Several weeks after that, I saw Uncle Dave and asked why he died when he did—why nothing could get him better. He said it was because he decided he would stay in the connection and refused to see the path to change the outcome. He was given countless opportunities to find a spouse who balanced him rather than choosing a person out of need or one he thought he could help, but he didn't take that path.

Looking back now on the experience of knowing and seeing my uncle's energy field change, I found similarities in others when I began reading professionally. It was also shown on some psychic readings with others that they could change their life path by getting balance within themselves. Uncle Dave's purpose was to see a balance and not feel he needed to be the one to fix another person. I later learned that the Earth ticket he was given was to hold love and light and to help balance humanity. He visited me before he reincarnated again to tell me he was coming back to get his love experience right and to be open to the soul who would be capable of love and not look for someone who would use him for rescue. I began looking through all the photos Uncle Dave brought to me and found a photo book of his tour in Vietnam. There were beautiful photos of the soldiers playing baseball and the children of the village laughing and having fun. I could feel the true happiness in the photos. I knew he was never intended to be here for war, and his involvement in the Army was against his true nature and only a human belief that humanity had fallen into.

The marriage history of Uncle Dave may feel familiar to you. You may have a relative who had a similar experience, or perhaps you might be reading the story and recognize a trait in yourself. Whether you marry for love or comfort, it makes a change in your energy field. The change can be positive or negative. If it's negative, it will take some clearing and making changes with choices to release it, and those that don't get changed in this life will be carried over for changes in the next until your soul masters the lesson. A negative reason to marry a person is to ensure they never leave you or to feel you will never be alone. As with any situation where you feel desperation, it should be evaluated so you can balance that need rather than carrying it into a marriage. When you carry that expectation into a marriage, the energy will feel lopsided, and in one way or another, the imbalance will continue to surface. If you're married to someone who is not a nice person, there's only so much your energy field can continue to take on before you're overloaded by their energetic stuff. If you've been married multiple times, you carry your last mate's energy into the connection unless you have cleared and reset an understanding of what is yours and what is theirs. When you take the time to look at what it is that you should take ownership of and change, there's a freeing effect you will feel when you finally release.

Now looking back at the list you made before of your outlook on marriage, what feelings do you have now? Do you feel equipped for a true love relationship, or do you feel you need a few more hard lessons before you can open for change?

Are you able to see why the people you first learned about marriage from may have had a skewed view of it, or was it perhaps a better view than what you have known? Do you see where their views came from? Do you agree with their beliefs, or have you formed your own view of the truth of the union of marriage? (See Figure 4.)

*Refer back to Chapter 1—Cord cleaning 101 if you feel the need to clear any unresolved relationship issues with a partner or their family

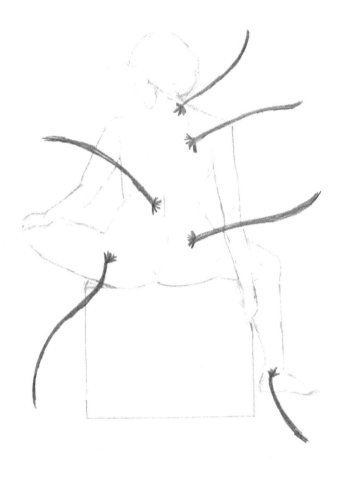

Figure 4—Relationship cords attached.

Chapter 6

The Abusers

Incarnation on Earth allows everyone to experience or witness abuse in some capacity, either toward themself or another. This has two effects that surface at the time of the experience. The first is that you see the need for cooperation as you recognize that everything is connected, and the second is that you learn how to raise your vibration. There's a crucial part in this on the spiritual level that often gets overlooked if you're sitting in the victim viewpoint. The experience is the subtle nudge for you to recognize the cooperative components that exist in all relationships in the Universe. You can't conceptualize dark without experiencing light. Change can't occur until a person understands their need and seeks a better path. Once this recognition happens, the person's energy field experiences a frequency upgrade, thus elevating the soul.

Now, to truly understand what has happened on Earth among humanity and why we are in the social coma that has come to be known as history, it's necessary to talk about the way early humans followed malicious beings who led them off track. The human experience of life on Earth wasn't designed as a time for people to hurt their brothers and sisters. It was meant to bring together pods of beings from all over the galaxy to one location to grow and learn from each other. This was intended to bring unity in a perfect utopia with humanity and allow all to have an experience where every group of represented beings chose to populate the planet with the experiment and mindset of oneness.

The push in the negative direction came from beings who knew of this and decided to visit Earth. They enjoyed how the human population was interested in what they may be missing out on and were open to the advice of the space travelers. These travelers were seen as angels even though they were not—they seemed to have flown here, or as it was written, fallen. The humans on Earth began to worship the travelers as gods and goddesses. As the travelers from other planets filled their egos by having humans worship them, it was the beginning of the end of the utopia that God created for us. The creator God gave us the freewill clause in our human agreement that would allow us to make our choices as we were guided. The freewill decisions humanity was making took many into the karmic cycle known today as the birth-to-death cycle of reincarnation. Some could still see the connection to the creator, but they became the victims of those who forged their own way with the guidance of the space travelers.

Those beings had already begun to destroy their own planet, and they enjoyed watching their influence take over humanity's thinking. Their teaching was that some individuals or groups should dominate over others. This was never God's choice for us, but as promised, we had free will. The fall of humanity began with the greed of those travelers. It seems humanity had a good run for several years before the intruders came. I'll go deeper on the intruders later in another book, but for now, let's stay focused on how the abuse began and why the imprint is still here.

When an action happens anywhere, anytime, there's an energetic imprint that stays in that area on Earth, or what I may refer to as that grid point. If the action is negative, the damaging energy stays there and can be felt for years after. If the energy is positive, it can be felt too. If there was an object involved in the abuse, such as a building or small item, it holds the frequency of the abuse. The tricky point of all this is that, when we have a lifetime where we either experience abuse or abuse another, it also stays in the energy field of our soul through every lifetime until it's cleared. The trauma that is held in the land, object, or energy field is not always easy to clear. Sometimes, the opportunity to do better in a similar situation is needed for the soul to clear it.

When there are imprints, they're not for God to clear. They're for humanity to clean by replacing them with love, light, and evolution of the human mentality. The evolution comes from raising our frequency by understanding ourself from an elevated viewpoint of a high heart perspective. The high heart connection is when the throat chakra and the heart are in sync. This happens when your heart is transparent, your emotions are uncovered, and the truth is what you are and live.

It was early summer, and as I always did when the weather felt great, I opened the windows to allow the breeze to flow through the house. The ringing of the phone was unexpected, as I hadn't set an appointment for anything early. It was a military officer I'd had a session with before who asked if I would spiritually investigate a coworker who was having difficulty with conflict in everyday work projects. As the officer handed the phone off to a man who I could feel wasn't really wanting to talk to me, I heard a door close behind him.

I introduced myself and asked his name. He waited a minute before answering and said, "Luis." I told him that I didn't force myself on anyone, so if he wanted to set something up when he was ready, I understood. Again, he sat there for a minute in silence. Then he asked, "What do you do?"

"Well, I listen to your question, and I parrot the response. The response is from God, spirit guides, angels, and sometimes your deceased loved ones, depending on what we want to know."

Luis explained that he'd made a career out of the military. He had several health issues. The military life he had chosen had brought him lots of adventure, travel, and a feeling of belonging that nothing in his life had given him before. Luis had married a woman before enlisting, and they had a daughter. His wife never liked traveling and refused to continue to move every time he was given orders and relocation was needed. His wife eventually returned to Argentina, and she filed for divorce. Luis had only seen his daughter twice after she and his wife moved back to Argentina. He'd served his country and had no family who cared to know how he was doing. The military served as a makeshift family for him. He explained that he had retired from the military, and he lived near the base and worked as a civilian.

Luis had attributed his back issues to his deployment during his military career. As I began to investigate his energy field, I was guided to regress him so we could see what needed to be recognized and released. I regressed in a way that allowed the individual to remain present and to hear all while offering to walk with them so I could keep a visual on things they perhaps didn't want to acknowledge. Doing this would ensure his best opportunity for release and healing.

I talked to him in preparation for the session and then began. The cross ventilation from the open windows in the house gave a relaxing feel to the session, and I could see by his energy he was more relaxed than when he was handed the phone. I wanted to see where the back issues originated from, so I began walking him back with me. We were standing in a kitchen, and he was six years old, shucking peas. I saw a smaller boy on the sofa who seemed to be four or five. They both looked malnourished. A woman I understood intuitively to be his grandmother had an aggravation about her regarding her position in life. The radio was playing, and the boy on the sofa was laughing and playing with a little monkey. Luis turned around to see his brother playing. It seemed the grandmother was unhappy that the boys were happy. As Luis laughed, the woman behind him got annoyed. The monkey seemed to do something even funnier, then the grandmother grabbed a large wooden spoon hanging on the wall and hit Luis across the back as hard as she could. His attention was on the monkey, so as he was struck with the wooden spoon, he lost his balance, and he and the bowl of peas hit the floor. She lifted the spoon and hit his back again. This time, the boy on the sofa turned off the radio and ran to Luis, trying to help him up. The grandmother somehow stopped herself from hitting him again and kicked him in his side. Luis was crying and trying to fight through the pain as he picked up the peas he'd been working on before they hit the floor. He continued to work on what he was given to do as his brother began helping him. There were no sounds in the room except the grandmother adding a lid to the pot and moving some things around.

I understood—that experience was the foundation of the back pain. I checked in on Luis's current energy, as we had just experienced something I was sure he'd forgotten about. He seemed good and was in as relaxed a state as he'd been in when we started the regression.

I glanced back at the scene from the doorway of his grandmother's kitchen. As I was looking around the room, God said, "This is a release that needs to happen for his back to feel better." I thought, *If this is* one *of the things that will help his back to feel better, then what's the other?* The breeze blew through the room, and as I briefly opened my eyes, a woman was there. She identified herself as Luis's mother and said she left him and his brother to go off with a man, and their grandmother raised them until she could send them to live with other relatives. Luis went to the United States at twelve and eventually joined the Army, while his brother stayed in Argentina.

I shared what I was hearing with Luis as we stepped back into his grandmother's house for the next emotional release. This time, it was the day he signed up for the Army. The recruiter who was visiting the home explained that once Luis became a member of the Army, he would have a sense of belonging and never regret his choice. The scene felt odd. The grandmother seemed relieved to finally be released of her responsibility for Luis, and while I watched, Luis's energy shifted too. It was because of the promise of always feeling he belonged and thinking he would never again experience the feeling of being unwanted. His mother stepped to my side while I was watching this interaction and said, "He felt unwanted by me, then my mother would hit him or make him work if she found him happy." I felt the frequency of God come in and say, "The grandmother hated caring for the boys, and in her feelings of being miserable, she didn't like it if they found any happiness or joy." The hit from the wooden spoon was an example. Luis was laughing, and she was bitter. The wooden spoon was used several times to hit the boys. The most happiness the boys experienced came at the times they were away from their grandmother's house.

The day Luis signed up for the Army, he felt like he belonged, and when the day of his retirement came, the fear of the rejection he'd experienced was coming back. The memories of the grandmother's abuse had not been forgotten, but since they were so long ago, he hadn't considered that they were where the pain in his back began.

As I invited Luis to leave his grandmother's house and return to the present moment, I saw a shift in his energy. I was guided by God's frequency that an acknowledgment was needed to give him permission to release. We chatted for a few minutes about how he felt. Luis confessed that the experience wasn't what he expected, and he was grateful. He told me his back was already feeling better. I urged him to take it easy and allow the energy to completely change over in his field so he could reset the new template that was being installed by his angels and spirit guides from the clearing that had taken place.

There are times when I've been in a session with a client, and it's shown to me that their abuse was a balancing experience so that they could understand firsthand why abuse was a wrongdoing in their past life. This type of balancing is something that an individual's higher self needs to experience so they can comprehend the feelings and hurt that may accompany abuse or trauma. If you've abused any living being—that includes humans, animals, and the Earth—and you didn't come to understand why what you were doing was wrong during your lifetime, then your soul will have to feel the experience as if it's happening to you. If you still seem to need extra understanding, then you'll incarnate into a life of experiences with that need embedded in your soul to invite higher understanding.

There's a reason why the wave of human consciousness has begun to come to the aid of animals. Evolved beings know that eating anything with a soul is wrong. Before man decided to live differently than the creator intended, we ate a vegetation diet, and the Earth provided all that we needed. The human body has changed over the centuries to adapt to the diet and lifestyle we have come to know today. It's crucial that if you see things in your life that you feel in your heart are wrong, you make the changes now so you don't have to experience the teachings of the soul in a profound, painful way.

When I decided to question why humanity eats meat, I never thought I would get a spiritual lesson along with a human history lesson. I was always completely disgusted when Mom would make meatloaf. I wouldn't eat it. We had pear and pecan trees in our backyard along with other things growing, so when I knew she was making something like meatloaf, I would eat from the yard so I wouldn't be hungry. When the COVID outbreak happened and I asked God what I was supposed to do, he said, "Begin by teaching those who are ready to learn as they are elevating up in their frequency, and those who are not ready must find their own way in another reincarnation."

The first thing he wanted me to do was teach the real reason animals came to Earth, which was to love and live in balance with humanity. The book we know as the Bible talks about sacrifices, which are not called for by the creator God. It was a being from another planet that requested it so they could see humans scurry around, trying to please them. God the creator doesn't need a human to sacrifice a lamb or a child. God could take them both from us in a second if needed. The Bible was written by man, not God. It doesn't mention much about how we were originally meant to live. It instead explains much that the visitors from other planets—the fallen angels—wanted us to do. The required sacrifices and conditions for living righteously mentioned in the Bible were the teachings of the visitors. Eating animals was taught by those visitors, and that lifestyle keeps us from fully obtaining the spiritual ascension that souls seek in every lifetime. God demonstrates no bias toward any one soul. The souls realize after they return to the light of God that they participated again in what they knew was wrong by eating the body of an animal, judging themselves or others, and seeing one church as their key to enlightenment. Humanity has continued to abuse themselves, each other, and animals.

It's time for the awakening to begin as many people begin to wake up and realize that the word they've been following wasn't the word of God but the word of those who liked seeing humanity fight each other. These are threads that have become embedded in our field from the families we came into and the beliefs we hold. These threads will continue to come out as we make our way to the higher frequency within our lifetime. The goal is to live free of needing to harm another and to protect our temple from the negative talk that was taught eons ago to hinder our life experience and our spiritual expansion.

When you realize you don't like the way you've been living, you can change it by teaching and influencing others toward a healthier mindset and life.

If you want to help animals, go vegan. Be the change in your family; be the change for the world.

The churches spent their early days condemning, and if you're disconnected from that belief, help others to release the judgment instilled by the church and embrace that they are accepted by God and they are loved. There should be no guilt. This is the secret to keeping and improving the current and future of humanity. There's no church needed to get you acquainted with a life with God. It happens within your heart—there's no middleman. You are an aspect of God, and you can never be separated, even if you tried.

Exercise #7

Refer back to Chapter 1—Grounding 101. At this point, you should start realizing your self-worth and the connection you have to the divine. Grounding allows you to connect to the divine stream of energy and reconnect to your higher self. For this exercise, keep yourself in a state of grounding for twenty to thirty minutes while *only* maintaining focus on breath, stillness, and visualizing the light within you. Practice this daily, and you will begin to establish an awareness of self within and beyond. You will soon realize that LOVE is all there really is.

Chapter 7

The Hookers

I've discussed hooks in my teachings before, so some of you may already be familiar with this term. When I was younger, seeing hooks in a field was startling since they look barbaric and should never be in the energy field. When they're present, it makes it nearly impossible to move beyond a certain point. We get stuck in situations attached to experiences in which the hooks became embedded to begin with.

I've talked about hooks I saw in energy fields early in my life, even when I had no idea why they were in an energy field. I only knew that they didn't belong, and when the hooks would stand out, they were often magnified as if I really needed to notice them. These were times I was learning so I would recognize what needed to be released and healed within the human experience. You may need to reference it as we dig deeper into understanding the energetic hooks.

When hooks appear in the energy field, they can be of various sizes depending on the reasons they are there (see Figure 5). The size will also indicate if the hook will be able to be removed in this lifetime. Sometimes when hooks are large, it takes a few go-arounds with different lifetimes for them to finally be released. The hooks can release on their own once the person has grown beyond the embedded ideas that put them there. The exercise below will help identify some of the hooks that have been embedded in your energy field. These hooks may release on their own once you've identified a person or situation that helped create them.

*Note: Gurus or energy workers may claim that they can remove these for you. No one else can remove hooks for you. The only way is to do it personally by changing your belief that you need someone else to survive or thrive in this life.

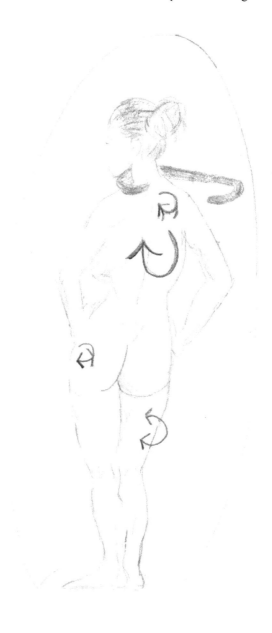

Figure 5—Energetic hooks of various sizes and placements.

The best example is when a person feels the only thing to focus on in this life is finding someone who can take care of them. This is a hard hook to remove in an energy field. There are usually two things that occur with this belief. One is that the person's higher self will decide that the only way for them to learn that they don't need someone is by a "foot sweep." Foot sweep is a common term in Tang Soo Do, Muay Thai, jujitsu, and karate. This move is basically knocking the person off their feet so they fall to the floor. It may also be seen as being brought to their knees. If you think about people who rose from a tough relationship or a situation of being cut off from their family only to go on to bigger things in life, a foot sweep was needed for those individuals to find out what they could accomplish on their own while releasing the belief that they needed another person to rescue them. The second teaching by the higher self may be to allow the individual to see examples of situations around them to give subtle nudges until the soul recognizes what it has been doing and decides to raise its frequency.

Energetic hooks are placed in the energy field of any living being that has been used, lured, bought, or brainwashed by any other living being.

<u>Exercise #8</u>

Now that you're aware of how energetic hooks come to be in the energy field, take time to list people who might have placed an energetic hook in your energy field. Please take your time on this. Really feel the energy around what comes to your mind. This needs to come from a place of truth and not anger.

(Example: Ex-husband threatened to take me to court for custody of my child)

1)_____

_____

2)_____

_____

3)_____

_____

4)_____

_____

6)_____

_____

7)_____

_____

8)_____

_____

9)_____

_____

10)_____

_____

There was a time after I realized what I could see and how I could see it that I started offering personal readings. Who needed the teachings wasn't for me to determine as I found out soon after I began offering readings to women in section eight subsidized housing.

While I was offering readings to some of these women, I still had regular clients. At times when I was reading for my clients, some of whom were very well off, I noticed they had similar lessons to those living in section eight housing. While their lifestyles were very different, the one underlying factor was that they wanted to find a man to support them—or in some cases, the word the women would use was to "save" them. The guidance I was given was if people continue to think of marriage or love relationships as the way of finding someone who will save them or be their provider, then neither person will ever be truly fulfilled on a spiritual level. When we come into life and it's impressed upon us by our family that we need to find a person to take care of us, then that's what we believe. This ideal was put in place so those who are of female identity would be inclined to see themselves as less than, and that is how it has continued to be for the experience of many on Earth.

Joseline came in asking only about a potential marriage with a guy she'd been with on a few occasions. He was president of a large automotive manufacturer, and I could see she was in love with his success, not his true personality. Joseline—who had a thriving career with a recognizable company making over $250,000 a year with commission—made a comment that she wanted to be married to have someone to take care of her so she would have plenty of money and a nice place to live. When I looked into her energy field, I noticed a few very large hooks. The big one was placed in the solar plexus and seemed to go all the way through to her back from what looked to be ten lifetimes ago. It looked barbaric—as if it were left from a lifetime of torture. The other two were in the head region, which appeared to be from this lifetime.

As soon as she said the comment, Quan Yin came in and identified as a volunteer to help in the female empowerment movement to balance the human life path experience. I was happy to see Quan Yin and asked, "Human life path experience?" Quan Yin was a vision of golden light that was mixed with a beautiful pink color. She was smiling, happy to communicate with me, and answered, "Yes, the human experience has been one-sided for what seems to be forever. That is changing—the old ways ingrained in the old mindset will die off, and a rebirth of balance will take place. Please continue to spread the word that balance happens from within, and when a soul is balanced, there are no deep lines drawn as to who saves who. It is all working together. That will be the true balance."

As I heard what Quan Yin said, I asked the client why she felt she needed someone to take care of her. She laughed at me as if I were silly and said, "I want a man to be able to buy me beautiful things and take me out to fancy places."

I still didn't understand why she felt that way, making the money she made. So I asked, "Do you not dine out at nice places? What does your home look like? Please tell me why you feel you lack money."

She was stunned by my questions and sat there in silence, just looking at me. Then she said, "You wouldn't understand because you haven't experienced the life I have, nor do you seem to care about having nice things."

Quan Yin stepped forward again, explaining to me that the woman in front of me would marry a man who was well off and still be completely miserable, wishing she hadn't married at all. After hearing Quan Yin, I looked at my client and said, "You will marry that man you want, and you will wish you never had, as you will be unhappy then too. There's nothing I can help you with since you know better than I what you need."

A few years had gone by, and Joseline called, explaining that she had married the guy she had been waiting for, and it was a complete mess. She told me they had so much of everything and traveled all over the world, drove fancy cars, and lived in a large home, and yet she was sad. He cheated on her, and while she was upset over his actions, she didn't want to leave the lifestyle. Every day, she thought about the happiness she'd had and was unable to recognize, feeling that being married was a reward that represented success. Quan Yin came forward and said she still had a couple of years of learning, but now she would discover humility and integrity. The next couple of years would be tough, but it was what her soul needed for spiritual growth. I asked for my own curiosity, "Why would you not just buy a house and set your life up the way you wanted it?"

She paused for a moment and told me that I wouldn't understand. I knew she had her own struggles and wasn't going to take guidance from Quan Yin or me. I was slightly annoyed by the fact that she called me and was still not ready to open to her truth, so I said, "Why did you call me?"

I could feel she was puzzled, too, then she said, "I wanted you to tell me that the relationship would work out and that he won't cheat on me again." At that moment, Quan Yin opened a portal showing Joseline's husband leaving to run to the store, then walking into a shady massage place and coming out after twenty minutes before heading to the store to get groceries. "He was cheating on his wife with you and is cheating on you now. There are no women he will ever be faithful to because he thinks he's entitled to anything he wants at any time. I think you want me to sprinkle some pixie dust on this to make it perfect for you, but that's not the lesson here. The lesson is very clear. Do you feel you live with integrity?"

"Yes, I do—I'm doing nothing wrong," she snapped back.

"I didn't say you did anything wrong, but you're cheating yourself out of being in a healthy relationship by choosing to continue with someone who obviously lacks integrity," I answered with the hopes something would spark truth with her. I went on to explain that when she decided she deserved truth and honesty, she would receive those things in another partner. I knew she knew he would never be faithful, so before ending the conversation, I said, "Life is never fun or happy when you're with someone you can't trust."

Chapter 8

The Loop

If you've watched my videos on TikTok or YouTube, you've heard me refer to loops in the energy field or repeating patterns during reincarnations that occur in a series. These are often lessons of self-growth. The experience could be something simple, like realizing self-courage, to perhaps something much more significant, like saving someone's life. The loop of an experience begins from a human's perspective as a missed opportunity. The missed opportunity may also be revisited later in life as perhaps a regret, but not always. It may be a passing thought of something you wish you would have done.

So what makes it a loop, you ask? It's a lesson or an experience that you took into calculation on your Earthly visit. When you weren't able to seize the experience, it was added on by your higher self as something you would try to achieve in the next life. Don't let the word *achieve* make you take a glance over all the big stuff you've done or passed on and think you understand. Sometimes, the things that are in loops are seen as very small through the human eye, or they may not be seen at all. When it comes to walking your path, you may not notice the small things you are to accept, conquer, or dismiss. To see those small things, you need a little quiet time sitting with yourself so that you can notice the most unnoticeable nuances. The subtleties of any situation are easily overlooked when you allow your human ego or hardheadedness to stay focused on ground-level living and forget to feel things out on a spiritual level.

Exercise #9

In the lines below, write down situations or patterns that you feel you may be repeating in this life. This can be a relationship type that you continue to be attracted to or something you continue to do to self-sabotage your good experiences.

Acknowledging these patterns is an important step in realizing that you can break the loop.

(Example: Continually dating abusive people, not speaking my truth)

1)

_____

_____

2)

_____

_____

3)

_____

_____

4)

_____

_____

5)

_____

_____

I began noticing loops when I read for a woman named Ashley who had come to me regarding a man named Kordell she claimed to be in love with. The man was a regular at a club she worked for. Ashley explained that her attraction was so insane, even she was beginning to question the hold he had over her. She explained that being with him "feels like home." As I asked Ashley to say his name, the spirit guides came in with a very firm message that she was not ready to walk away from him and would need another experience to warn her. Her spirit guides said the man she was asking about choked her in their last lifetime together after they made love. It wasn't planned in his mind—it was a fear-based action to keep her from being with anyone else. He thought if he couldn't have her, no one could. In this life, he still felt a sense of owning her. I sat there in silence for a moment when I saw her spirit guides open the view of Ashley in her last life with Kordell. Ashley was an African American slave, and Kordell was a white slave owner. He had many slaves but was in love with Ashley. She had known him since she was a child and had been raised working on the farm. Ashley and Kordell would sneak off to be with each other, and Ashley's family was aware of what was happening. Ashley's family was planning to leave. Ashley knew of the plan, so the last night she knew she would be with Kordell, after they made love, she told him that she didn't see the relationship changing and that he should pursue someone else, as that was her plan. He told her no, and as she began to try to close the conversation, he reached up and choked her to death. He took off from their meeting spot and left her lying there. As I was shocked by what had been shown to me, I realized I might have sat in silence for too long. Then I heard Ashley repeatedly ask what I was seeing. I told her what the spirit guides had just shown me, then one of her guides said, "Kordell chokes her now as part of their sexual experience and will kill her in this life the same way if she doesn't get away from him."

My heart was beating hard after the visual and warning. I blurted out, "Ashley! I know he tries to choke you when you're intimate, and that's how he's going to kill you in this life if you don't stop seeing him." Her spirit guides told me to tell her that she'd had a few lives with him where their experiences ended with her being choked to death. I then continued to parrot what the spirit guides were showing me and said, "Ashley, you need to know he has choked you a few times, and the name he chose to carry in life means rope maker or cord maker. The spirit guides told me."

As I explained what I'd seen, she was in shock, then she told me, "He told me it turns him on to act like he's choking me. The weirdest part of all that you're telling me is that he's part African American and part Caucasian, and I'm Caucasian." It didn't surprise me that there had been a flip of ethnicity between them because which ethnicity you incarnate with depends on what you're here to learn. If it's important for you to learn from an ethnicity you didn't accept or understand before, then your soul may decide that incarnating as that particular one will help you in your new lifetime. The culture, the location, and the ethnicity are purposely chosen for that life you are going into. She seemed to understand and thanked me for the session.

The guides then said, "While you're warning her now, she is too hardheaded to break away yet—but she will."

A few months went by when I got a call from Ashley. I could tell by her tone she was excited to have reached me. She sounded different than she had before. She asked if I remembered her, and as I thought about the past life scene, the warning, and the loop, I answered, "Of course I remember you."

She said she listened to what I told her in our session but never really felt he would do anything. She admitted that when he needed money, he would come by the club and get some from her, so she thought he would never hurt her since she helped him frequently. Her tone became serious, then she explained that after work one day, Kordell came home with her. Ashley's mom, Darlene, who she lived with, helped out by babysitting her three-year-old granddaughter while Ashley worked. While she and Kordell were in the bedroom, he went into the choke move that he loved, and after she tried to get him to stop, she woke up with her mom crying and screaming over her body. After getting a glass of water, Ashley asked, "What happened?" Her mother explained that she was watching TV in the living room when Kordell ran from the bedroom half-dressed, not saying a word, and drove away. Darlene felt something was off and ran to check on Ashley when she found her unresponsive and called 911. She could feel a pulse and tried to get her to wake up. Ashley said, "Kordell thought he'd killed me, and after remembering what you told me, I'm now taking it seriously." She told me she worked another week and took my advice about how she should work at a car dealership until she finished school for a certification. She was now working for a car dealership, had moved to a new place, and had broken the loop with Kordell, who happened to be a karmic soul mate.

Chapter 9

The Admission

The energy field carries an imprint of trauma and connections that go way beyond our human perception of reality. It really stems from what is embedded from past lifetimes here and on other planets. This is a warped view from previous lifetimes and situations we have incarnated into so we could get a well-rounded education from the Universe as a whole. Sometimes when looking into a soul, there will be many things that open and begin to show as experiences that the individual has chosen to have.

Let's start by looking into our own soul's adventures. The best way this is done is from a third-person viewpoint. Think of a counselor or psychiatrist. If you've never met with one in person, then think of one you've seen in a movie or show. The counselor or psychiatrist normally listens and nods while keeping the questions simple to allow the subject to understand. By asking straightforward questions and nodding, it allows the client to expand in their own words what their feelings are and why they are there to begin with.

I want you to be in the most honest place possible. There's no one to judge you. The answers will only help you purge all that's preventing you from being the best version of yourself and raise your frequency now. When you begin to raise your frequency, you're able to release stuff you've held on to in an easier way than confronting big issues that cross your path to help you grow.

Exercise #10

You're now going to do an exercise where you act as your own counselor. I want you to think about the words below and circle those that apply to you. Take the perspective of an outside observer who is looking at you from an objective point of view. Think of how that person would see you. Please circle the items on the list that they would notice. Don't think of your best friend or family member, just an unbiased person. We want to believe certain characteristics about ourselves that may not be the way others see us. Have you been told something you didn't like to hear about yourself by more than two or three people? This is an exercise for self-awareness and can help to clear negative embedded imprints.

Non-judgmental   Loyal   Careless   _____

Kind   Arrogant   Independent   _____

Caring   Jealous   Humble   _____

Hateful   Courageous   Dependent   _____

Prejudiced   Vindictive   Conceded   _____

Complacent   Hard-working   Materialistic   _____

Selfish   Trustworthy   Rude   _____

Honest   Lazy   Creative   _____

Loving   Self-confident   Stubborn   _____

*Feel free to add any other characteristics that are not listed and circle them.

While still looking at the list through the eyes of someone who knows you, give an example of why you see yourself as the descriptive words you circled. You will probably want to return to this more than once and reevaluate it. Is there something listed you would like to become? What's stopping you? Is it the view that another person impressed upon you? Is the view from a faith or belief?

When we evaluate ourselves, we may be tempted to justify everything we ever did. Our views of good and bad are perceived notions that we were taught in some fashion during our formative years. These views, regardless of where we're from or what lifetime we're in, can play a major role in the experiences that our higher self calls in for us.

We have experiences to help raise our frequency and release any views of ourselves as lacking the ability to move forward in the way our soul desires to live. When we've had lives in which we were unable to master the mindset to help a whole or a part of us return to our origin, the cycle will continue. This is called a karmic loop— when a situation continues to play out in the same way over and over until the soul says, *I am going to overcome this and break the cycle.* The cycle can be for various lessons; some of those I've seen included abandonment, murder, abuse, victimization, or being a user.

Think about your own life in just this lifetime. Is there a pattern with relationships? Are there certain types of friends or lovers you continue to attract? Sometimes you may attract people who fit the same relationship styles you were used to in your family of origin. If you think about those who attract narcissistic people, you'll notice the pattern will continue to repeat until the lesson is learned. So you may be asking, when and how is the lesson learned? It's learned when you're no longer drawn in by them.

Humanity has shifted from the God-consciousness, meaning that humans who existed on the Earth once had a very clear knowledge of God and memory of experiences from other lifetimes in places other than the Earth. When humans decided to go outside the plan, it was all on them to find their way back to the original plan. That has been tricky because now, when we enter a new lifetime, we forget the pitfalls we learned before.

We have certain fears that we're either born with or that come up at various times in our lives, sometimes through things we experience. There are also times when fear or anxiety come up for no clear reason.

A few years back, my daughter Breezy and I had lunch at California Pizza Kitchen. Although it was lunchtime, it wasn't packed. Breezy had lost her voice. It wasn't painful, only bothersome. One of the languages she happens to be fluent in is ASL, so while she had been without a voice, she used sign language to communicate. The hostess seated us, and the waitress approached the table. She was friendly and introduced herself while offering to get our drinks. I told her I would have a tea, then Breezy signed to me her preferred drink, and I relayed it to the waitress. As soon as I finished telling the waitress our drink order, her energy shifted to a dark orange color all over her body. She did a walk-run to get away from the table as if she were scared to death. She came back to the table, only making eye contact with me, and took the order. When the food came out, it was delivered by another server. As I watched her handle her only other table, she pointedly avoided ours. We needed drink refills, but I knew there was no chance of getting her back to the table, so I walked up to the counter to get them myself.

As I finished eating, the frequency of God came in, saying, "She is frightened not by what you have done but by who she was and what she did." Okay, but at that point, I needed to pay the tab, and after trying to get her attention for fifteen minutes, she still made sure not to make eye contact. Another server passed our table, and I asked if he could let our server know we were ready to pay the tab. I watched as he told her, and she still refused to look over at us.

My lunch break was well beyond over, and I was at the point of needing to approach the counter to pay the tab. I knew by the server's energy field she was afraid of anyone who had a disability.

When I walked up, a woman there asked how she could help me. I told her the waitress took our drink and food order, but once she saw that my daughter couldn't talk and used sign language, she refused to acknowledge us and never came back to the table. Then I gestured to the server I flagged down and explained I had asked him to tell her we needed the tab. By that point, Breezy had gotten up from the table and walked to the door to wait for me. The manager noticed our waitress, who was approaching the table to pick up the plates. Then the manager looked at me and said, "I'm sorry for the service you received. That server doesn't represent the values we hold here at CPK."

As I was watching the manager pull up the ticket, I was told by her spirit guides that a similar situation had happened before with the same waitress. The manager carried a beautiful green energy in her field and was truly concerned about the experience we'd had. I handed her my credit card, and she refused to accept it, telling me lunch was on her.

After we left, I sat and thought about the experience. As I did, Archangel Sandalphon came in to explain that when a soul causes harm that results in a being, whether animal or human, being left with a disability, then in their next life, the soul experiences the pain but will struggle to understand it. If the soul's higher self believes that feeling the emotional and physical struggle wasn't enough, then the soul might choose a life with a disability to learn from. When that happens, they usually choose parents and guardians who have something to learn from the experience too. The fear that comes up for people who are afraid of those with disabilities needs to be cleared so that acceptance and understanding can come from a place of love. If the fear is not elevated and dissolved by the light of love, then the marking will be in the energy field, and to remove it, a lifetime of that disability may need to be experienced. It's love and acceptance that will clear the fear away. When there's love presented in place of fear, then the fear is dissolved.

Archangel Sandalphon's energy was a streaming frequency of higher education and reaching beyond the veil of understanding. The first time I saw him, I was working in a shop for a woman named C.J. (I talk more about that time in my life in *How I Found My Superpowers*). He came in during some energy work I was doing on a client named Alan, who could barely walk without getting winded. Alan was a six-foot-four, slender, sixty-three-year-old cowboy whose overall energy color was pink with darkness around the throat and chest area and a filter around the solar plexus. If he parked ten feet away, it might take him fifteen minutes to get to the door of the shop. The treatment room had a ten-foot-tall ceiling, and it wasn't enough space for Sandalphon. I could only view the top part of his body in that ten-foot space—from the top of his head to the middle of his rib cage—and he filled the room. I knew he must have had another ten feet to his being and was just trying to accommodate me so I could see him.

He'd appeared after I placed my hands on each side of Alan's head. Sandalphon opened a space where I saw Alan as a small boy. His mother was taking what appeared to be a boom bristle that she had broken off and was dipping it in gasoline. She then took the bristle and put it on Alan's tonsils. My legs felt as if they might buckle, then Sandalphon streamed energy into both of us. That moment was the root of the reason he was experiencing breathing difficulties along with lung and throat issues. The session was silent, and I continued to watch what Sandalphon was doing, as it was different from what I had witnessed before that point.

I don't remember most of the end of the session, only that I felt we both received healing. When Alan sat up from the table, he said he felt better, then he stood up. As he looked at the wall for a moment, he said, "I recall something I haven't thought about in years."

"I saw something too—what did you see?" I asked. At that point, Alan knew nothing of what I could see, only that I offered Reiki. Alan slipped his foot back in his boot and reached for the other one. I knew he didn't want to tell me. He stood and reached for the doorknob.

At that point, I felt Sandalphon's beautiful energy, but he seemed to be leaving through the same portal he came in. As he left, he was urging me to tell Alan the throat story.

I stepped forward and said, "Alan, I saw you as a boy with your mom, then I saw her take a broom bristle and drip a drop of gasoline onto your tonsils."

He looked at me, not quite believing what he was hearing. If anyone else had mentioned the spirit world to him, he might have laughed, but there was a spark of what I knew that he wanted to talk about. He finally spoke. "Yeah, I saw that too. How did you see that? Why did that memory come up?"

I tried to think quickly since I had one chance to help him open, and if I freaked him out too much, he might run for good. "You wanted to have energy work to help you in healing your breathing issues, and the memory that came up is directly attached to the breathing issues."

"My mom was doing what she thought would help me at the time," he said, trying to stand up for his mom as if that were the thing we were focused on.

"That's not the thing that was healed by showing us that situation. It was the reason why you had so many infections in the throat that I was to look at, which was connected to your father, not your mother. Your father did some horrible things that he took joy in seeing you get upset over, and you learned you couldn't tell him when you were upset because he would do more of what upset you. This is what closed you down from speaking your truth to him and the cause behind the throat issues."

"Did you see anything else?" he asked.

"Yes, Archangel Sandalphon was here and showed me your father and some of the things he did." Alan hung his head a bit, and I could still see him trying to process what had happened. I was watching the shift happening in his energy field. He opened the door as I watched his energy continue to shift. He made pleasantries with C.J., and she commented on him being able to walk at a better pace.

I learned that the soul carries situations that can eventually move into the body and cause disease, and when the situations are recognized from different perspectives, great changes occur for the better.

Chapter 10

The Religion

We as humans have fallen into the holding pattern of following religious beliefs and practices and not stopping to question any of them. Some of these beliefs have kept us trapped in the three-dimensional mindset and have never allowed us to crawl out from underneath the avalanche of lies and misguided beliefs we continue to worship.

Proverbs 13:24 (NIV) says, "Whoever spares the rod hates their children, but the one who loves their children is careful to discipline them."

This was a belief from a human perspective that was shared in the Bible. The Bible contains the traditions of men that were handed down through the years before being written and translated.

Religion has played a key role in the guilt humanity carries and puts on each other. It has been the self-ladened burden that echoes through history and is the number one reason why so many hold on to self-judgment. It's the most crippling hand-me-down that we as humans have gifted each other since the beginning when religion and spiritual beliefs were first practiced on Earth. No one is immune from the imprint that the soul carries from old religious beliefs that have been laid upon us to either control, ridicule, or destroy those who were seen as heart-centered, wise, and unable to be brainwashed. The religious remnants often stay tethered to the soul regardless of what spiritual beliefs you identify with in this life. If you identify with none of the spiritual views floating around today and claim to be agnostic or atheist, you're still not cleared from those stored encounters from other lifetimes. Sometimes when I've sat to do a psychic reading for a person distraught over the religion they grew up in, I see that the conflict may have come up so the individual can awaken in this life and break the etheric cords that have bound them for repeated lifetimes.

Most of the population can't imagine having a life outside of what they've experienced, and many can only envision the worldview placed on them by someone in their family based on that person's opinion or religious views. I've had sessions with people who seem to believe that if they are Hindu in this lifetime, all their lives have been Hindu Indian. The same happens with Christians and people from any other group. This belief is usually based on the prejudice taught by many in the community. It's sometimes so drenched with prejudice that they can't see beyond to grasp the meaning of life, which is acceptance and love for all.

Exercise #11

Please use the space below to write about how religion was introduced to you as a child or a teen. If you grew up in a home that didn't practice or believe, then write the words attached to your understanding when you first encountered a religion or explanation of one.

Let's start with a few words or lines that come to mind about your first information on religion. Please don't overthink your answers— they are for self-reflection only.

(Example: Local church members dropped off a bag of candy inviting me to church on Sunday,

I watched my mother reading the Bible every night before bed)

Katharine Branham

1)

_____

_____

_____

_____

2)

_____

_____

_____

_____

3)

_____

_____

_____

_____

4)

_____

_____

_____

_____

5)

_____

_____

_____

_____

6)

_____

_____

_____

_____

7)

_____

_____

_____

_____

8)

_____

_____

_____

_____

9)

_____

_____

_____

_____

10)

_____

_____

_____

_____

When I was nine years old, I had a friend from dance class named Stephine whose family members were devoted Catholics. She had five siblings. When her parents worked, she was watched over by her teenage sister Latisha. Latisha resented having to watch her siblings, so when she did, she ruled with an iron fist. The house was spotless when the parents got home since the siblings cleaned from the time they came home from school until their parents returned at eight. When one of the siblings had something else to do, it would anger Latisha, and she would take bottle caps and line them along the wall four inches out. She would then have the sibling she felt needed to be punished kneel on those bottle caps for the length of time they were off doing something else. The bottle caps were the kind you need a bottle opener for, and they were sharp. She would use a wooden ruler and kitchen timer to keep it uniform. This went on for a year, and when the siblings would try to tell their parents, Latisha would take it out on them when she watched them the next day. There was no one else to watch them, and they felt stuck.

Stephine's mom came home early from work one day. She peered through the side window next to the door to see if the kids were in the den only to find two of them kneeling on bottle caps, facing the wall. Surprised and curious, she opened the door, asking what they were doing. Stephine told her mom she was being punished for her dance class, and anytime she had a class and couldn't clean the house, she had to kneel on bottle caps. Her mother, shocked, asked Latisha why she decided that was okay to do to her brothers and sisters. She said, "It's not fair they have activities since I have to babysit every day during the week."

"Whatever gave you the idea this was something you should do?" her mom questioned.

"The nuns make us do this at school when they think we're disobedient," she answered.

This was the reason Stephine's family decided to take the kids out of Catholic school. They continued to go to church, and it was a matter of time before they would finally break away. The imprint of the church went well beyond the bottle caps lesson for Latisha. It was the calculated precision of the punishment mentality placed upon humanity.

When a person is instilled with fear on any subject or in any way, it takes incredible strength to push past it. Much of what has been taught on a fear level within the churches is used to maintain

171

control. It's no surprise some identify as atheist since, on a certain level, they instinctively know the biblical teachings are not from creator source energy. The most interesting are the religions that promise if you do certain things, you'll have a fleet of virgins or that only those in the celestial kingdom will live in God's presence.

I was surprised to discover that when we reincarnate, it's not God sending us back in another incarnation to make us suffer. It's our own soul that makes the choice so we can perfect our learning until we are unmoved by man's teachings. As humanity realigns to its true origins, souls will know their connection to God from the start. No one can remove that connection or make it better through a sacrament, marriage, or bringing forth offspring. We are here to be good shepherds of the Earth and to get our beings heart-centered in love and light. This requires purging all that has felt like guilt, fear, and hate.

I received a call from another psychic who was having trouble with a man who refused to go into the light after his passing. When I was able to visit with the spirit, I learned he had been a preacher. He grew up in the Bible belt and could recite the Bible by heart. Since he was a man who believed in God and knew of heaven, it puzzled me why he wouldn't go into the light. "My name is Katharine. What's your name?" I asked.

"My friends called me Brooks." He smiled and seemed happy to talk to me.

"There's nothing to be afraid of in heaven. Why won't you go into the light?" I said, hoping he may say, "Oh yeah, you're right," and go. Instead, he began to explain that when he began his ministry as a young man in his early twenties, his examples were fire-and-brimstone preachings. He taught that way so he could scare the folks into doing what was best for their souls.

"If you felt you did the right thing, then your teachings of fire and brimstone should set you up nicely on the other side," I said, knowing I would hear words of regret.

"Well, at the time, that type of teaching was the example I had to go by. It was believed in the Bible community that if people weren't afraid, they would never do what's right. The days the collection plate needed to be filled, I did a sermon on hell and what they needed to do to avoid that place. So when the collection plate came around, out of guilt, they would toss extra money in."

I saw Archangel Azrael come in at that moment. Brooks saw him too.

"There's nothing to fear on the other side. Whatever you feel guilty about is the part of you that knows it was wrong. Your higher self will help you to understand a heart-centered way to help souls in the future."

He seemed to be mournful and asked if I would walk across with him.

"Archangel Azrael is here to walk with us. I'll walk across and come back to show you it's safe, then you can go across. Would that be helpful to you?"

As I said that, I noticed a part of his soul come back. I looked at Azrael and received the message that the soul piece that returned was the piece that had been terrified at a young age. Archangel Azrael stood next to Brooks, letting him know he was safe. As I walked over, experiencing the weird sensation of crossing, I could see the happiness of his soul. I smiled and said, "Look, I'm doing it again, Brooks," as I walked into the light and back over to him. I repeated this action a few times, then he was ready.

Before he stepped forward, he asked, "Is there a hell?"

"Not in the way it's presented in the Bible or in churches. The hell that I've witnessed is the hell that your higher self feels you need to experience to understand and learn. It's not a burning pit as it's depicted. The only time I knew of a soul feeling burned was when they purposely burned any living thing, including a person or animal. The experience is given so the soul knows not to do that again and is able to feel what that being experienced. If a soul has caused pain and suffering but recognizes it deep in their heart and is sorry for it and moves through their life changed in their ways and teaching others, the wrongs are cleared. If it's not recognized during that lifetime and a soul passes, then their higher self will have them experience the pain a few times over, and perhaps they may need to reincarnate in a life where it will be experienced as well. Whatever pain and suffering a soul inflicts on another living being, they will experience it themselves. Not going into the light doesn't prevent that from happening. Being outside the light feels incredibly lonely and dark." He seemed pleased and began walking to the light portal, accompanied by Archangel Azrael.

Brooks has not been the only preacher, minister, or priest I've watched cross or talked to after their death. It was shown to me that this is a perfect example of humanity continuing to teach fear, then realizing it's not the way. God's frequency came in and said, "The only way to teach and live is through the heart."

Katharine Branham

Chapter 11

The Father

The "sins of the father" was a phrase I'd heard several times from various people in different scenarios. It appears several times in the Bible. The term references ancestral sins. This means that what your grandfathers and grandmothers did will affect you. This is true in a sense. When a woman carries a child or a man fathers a child, the imprints of their actions to karma in their field are imprinted on the offspring. Our ancestors' sins or actions are embedded in our souls until we clear them.

Though it mentions the impact our ancestors have on us, the Bible doesn't emphasize that some of the residue of what you have

176

done will affect your children and your children's children. In order to break the loop and the imprinted action, you have to do better. You must purge your energy field by questioning why exactly your beliefs and traditions are practiced. Are they heart-centered? Did another living being suffer for your beliefs? Did another living being give its life for your traditions? What exactly are you doing, and is it heart-centered?

When we are heart-centered, there's no place for ego. The ego begins to get squeezed out, and the takeover of love in every direction begins to happen. It's then that we can let go of some of the things our ancestors participated in that went against a peaceful life on some level of existence. The old energy will be released by our energy field and transmuted by the light. Thus, we change the loop or negative karma the family has taken on. If you think back to Marcus's story in Chapter 2, the loop of low-level-dimension existence and alcoholism didn't imprint in his energy field since his soul was clean, so that wasn't a practice he needed to clear.

Years back, I met a woman named Treasa who was very much into her traditions. Her home was called "little Spain" by her family. The pictures of her father and uncles who had participated in the running of the bulls were proudly displayed on her walls as though they were great accomplishments. She even had a dried ear of a bull her father cut off after a bullfighting event where the bull was killed, and many men had gathered around, smiling in celebration. Her father cut the ear off as a souvenir of the day.

On the day of our session, she expressed not wanting to live anymore and said that when she looked back on her life, there had been very little true happiness. She asked, "Can you tell me if I have a curse?"

"Why do you feel you are cursed?" I asked, knowing it would give me the opening to help her in her own realization.

"I have been provided for, but I have not felt true happiness."

I realized I was being nudged by Archangel Raphael to ask her about the pictures on the wall and the family members in the photos. "Who are the men in the photos with the bulls on your wall?"

She smiled and said, "They are all my family. They would participate with great honor, and it became a tradition in my family."

I noticed another photo. It was a family photo, and the man looked like her. Archangel Raphael said, "That is her son with his family."

The woman looked at the photo, then explained that her son, Emanuel, didn't embrace the family traditions, and it was hurtful to her. "He is a doctor, you know," she stated with a smile.

Seeing that I needed to pull more information, I said, "You must be proud—he seems so happy, and he has a beautiful family."

She began to cry and said while she was happy her son was successful, he didn't embrace his heritage, which was important to her family.

"How many family members do you have?" I asked, knowing the son and his family were all she had left that she was close to.

"I have six people in my family still living."

At that point, Archangel Raphael was gesturing for me to ask about the man in a large oval gold-rim-framed photo that hung on the wall. "Who is that?" I asked while motioning to the distinguished image.

"That is my father," she responded with a smile, her eyes glossing over with tears. As I guided her to sit down, she explained that her family always found a way, but they suffered so much sadness. "Emanuel never seemed to embrace the family traditions, and that was hurtful to me since family traditions are important to maintain."

"Do you feel any negative energy when you look at the photos you have hanging?" I asked while waiting for a shift to happen in the energy field.

In a calm voice, she answered, "Yes, I feel my family's struggle to provide."

I could see she was looking from the view of the victim as the family traditions were being rejected by Emanuel. "This is way more than Emanuel rejecting the acceptance of the family traditions. This is the emotional sadness you feel from your own choices."

Archangel Raphael stepped next to her and motioned for me to allow her the process of the discovery. So I asked, "What beings do you see in the group photo?" She named all the men in the photo. I wanted her to mention the bull, which was an involuntary member of the event. She was still looking at the photo, so I asked, "What about the bull?"

She looked at the photo, and tears began to pour out faster than I could look for tissues. I looked around the room and eventually found the bathroom and grabbed toilet paper. It had only been a minute, and when I returned to the room, she had taken the photo down and began an even deeper cry. I handed her the toilet paper, and she said, "How could I have been so dumb? I never asked why the family decided it was a great day to watch a bull die in pain. My son used to say that the life our family had wasn't for him, and he had no connection to the traditions. That would hurt me because, on a certain level, I wished I could have been so strong not to accept the ways of my family." As we sat there talking, she was uncoiling the imprint that had been placed in the energy field since birth. The imprint was ridden with sadness and despair that the family had taken on from the things they called traditions—the despair the soul essence felt by partaking in something they deeply knew to be wrong.

I was grateful she was having the breakthrough while she was still here in this life and before it was her day to cross. The spirit of some of her deceased loved ones came in and explained that while they were here in this life, they did what they were taught and never questioned, even at times when it made them sad to see a bull die. The deceased family explained that when the sadness would creep up from within them, they would drink the night away. Her father explained how not recognizing it was wrong was a lesson he had to learn for his soul to prepare to evolve in the next lifetime. I was shown how his soul felt the fear, struggle, and painful death that that bull endured. And it wasn't just one bull—it was all the races and bullfights that he witnessed, cheered, and promoted to others. Not only was his energy field soiled with the blood of the bulls, but so were the energy fields of those he fathered. Emanuel was the beautiful soul who came in and questioned the methods and traditions that the family celebrated. He was able to break the karmic loop for the lineage moving forward.

What had happened in her family that day should not be seen as sad. It was to be celebrated, as the soul's lesson was learned. When it was time for me to go, there wasn't one picture left hanging that had a deceased animal in it, and the dried bull ear was taken down too. I saw the energy field shift to a great frequency. Treasa said, "I am going to redecorate my home from the bullfighting decor to something cheerful to shift the energy of the room. Emanuel always called my house the grotto due to the dark colors and Spanish decor. He will gladly help me in clearing all this out."

Breezy and I were out having lunch one day at a local taco spot. The owner was seldom there, but his father, Trent, was the manager and would make sure he would walk around to every table, greeting the guests. My lunch break wasn't long, so when we got there, we ordered right away, then walked outside to find a table in the sun so I could clear my energy a little before the food was served. Trent loved chitchatting with the tables. He didn't understand what I did for work—he might not have known that I worked at all. My lunch break was an important time for me to relax between sessions and not engage in conversations regarding anything that resembled work.

As he approached the table, I felt Breezy's energy shift into protective mode. While Breezy was completely unable to hide her emotions, she sensed when something could possibly infringe on our lunch and was able to pick up on any situation that could turn into work for me. It was usually people who would ask what I did, then want me to read for them right then and there—as if my lunchtime wasn't important.

Trent asked how our day was going, and then he began to tell us about a family that his family was close to who all died within the last week. Without us being able to stop him, he continued to talk about how the parents had died due to unrelated, random events, then the couple's adult son had accidentally shot himself. He went on to explain that the man had been cleaning his rifle when it went off. I could tell Trent was just shocked over the news and was still trying to process it. I didn't like the fact that he was using my lunch to do it. As he was talking about the gun accident, it was shown that the parents and the son all had imprints in their lineage that were supposed to be cleared in this lifetime, but they weren't on the trajectory to do so. The parents began hunting with the boy when he was young and allowed him to practice shooting raccoons that they had put food out for. This continued well into his teens, and it continued with more than raccoons. In fact, the parents would laugh at how many animals the boy put in the trash. The animals were brought to the attention of the family to help them evolve and change, but they had become so ingrained in the lifestyle they could no longer see beyond. I noticed the parents' souls would not only experience the pain they inflicted on animals, but they would also experience the sadness of the neighbors who lost pets to their son's shenanigans.

As Trent was still talking, I saw the gun go off and shoot the son in the face. When I asked God, "Why did he die in that way?" it was shown that was how the son's higher self chose to go so he would carry the mark on his face in the next life as just a small part of the soul lesson that lay before him on his spiritual path. As I could still feel God's energy, I asked, "Will this break the lineage in the family now that the son chose to die in such a way?"

"No, it will allow the soul to experience the pain, so in the next life, he knows how the animals felt that he tortured."

Now I wondered about the family, and I asked God, "Is the torture he will feel the only way?"

The frequency came in as quick as I asked and said, "No, when there is an ending to a family, there's usually a restart. The higher self of that soul seeks to go into the next life so they can get their soul perfected."

I could feel Jesus join and say, "When a family continues to stay stuck in their three-dimensional views and changes need to be made, there are many chances given. The higher self for each induvial wants to change, and it's for the heart to see what's right and do that. The imprint can't be removed until the old ways are cleared and a new mindset is established."

Then a scene opened with the son who shot himself in the face, and after his soul passed and he greeted God's light, the son's higher self took him in to review his life. As the son watched and calculated the number of animals he killed or tortured, the higher understanding opened a light from the center of his body, and he began feeling every torture he had put an animal through along with every cruel death. Then when I thought his soul could take no more, there was more. I thought it had gone on for fifteen minutes, but the God frequency came in and said, "His experience is much longer than the time you are watching, as some of the animals he tortured lived for days, and some endured a painful life because of him injuring them when they had no means for a healthy recovery. He will feel the pain for as long as is needed until he understands. This is a form of school for the soul."

I was finally able to get Trent to leave the table. By then, our food was sitting there cold, and I had to get back to the house. It was the last time that I visited that restaurant. I knew when I left that the place would be closing soon.

The lunch visit required me to go and ground because of the conversation with Trent. There will be times you may have a conversation that bothers you or times you feel lingering energy from another person. You will need to ground in order to disconnect yourself from the energy. When I read for someone, I clear myself afterward by walking with the intent to dispel the energy I picked up, and I ground to reset my field so I can stay clean.

Think of a person who may have confessed something to you. In order to alleviate their energy field, they have now offloaded something into your energy field. This is a subtle way of using you without you knowing what's happening. If you are in a career field where it's common to hear secrets and confessions, it's expected, but it still needs to be cleared. This would be another situation in which you should ground.

As a final point, I would like you to go to the first list that you made in the book. Notice that it may seem short compared to the lists you may make now. When glancing back at the first list of people, think about the energy attached to the emotions you had when you wrote them down. Did the energy shift and alleviate the hurt emotions? You will recognize that as you clear, the emotions become lighter. If an emotion continues to come up after you have cleared, it's usually a signal that the thread wasn't ready for release. You may need to hold the emotion for a while longer as the soul continues to process the lesson. When the clearing has been done right, no negative emotions should arise. You will have new eyes when it comes to understanding what energy is and is not. This is an important teaching to help you to clear during times of depression or imbalances when you have no idea why you feel that way. Humanity will increase its ability to see the energy field as we continue to awaken, and we will understand how easy it is to collect other people's shit in our energy field. Now that you are conscious of the people, activities, and places that can invade your energy field, it will be easier for you to clear it and move forward on your path.

In our next *SELF HELP SLUT* series workbook, *Getting to the Root of it All*, we will be discussing: *Surviving the shit that hasn't killed you.*

The Author

Bestselling author of *How I Found My Superpowers: An Introduction to the Spirit World.*

Katharine Branham is a Free-flowing Psychic Medium. She can tap into the Spirit World without blinking an eye. She has incredible gifts that seemed to be inherited at birth and several that she learned along her spiritual journey.

Many of her gifts are considered Superpowers by most, although Katharine explains that anyone can learn to find their own Superpowers. These Superpowers include open channel, remote viewer, clairvoyant, clairaudient, clairsentient, energy healing, and medical intuitive.

Katharine grew up in Houston, Texas and currently lives in The Woodlands where she participates in animal rights and rescue. She has two children, four furry babies, and enjoys tap dancing and hula hooping. Katharine's life mission is to help humanity return to their natural blueprint and awaken within.

You can find out more about Katharine at :

www.katharinebranham.com

or

www.psychickatharinebranham.com.

Also by Katharine Branham

Coming Soon

Available where books are sold.

Katharine Branham

CPSIA information can be obtained
at www.ICGtesting.com
Printed in the USA
BVHW092225280622
640819BV00013B/1211

9 781956 925012